Photographing
BUTTERFLIES
AND OTHER INSECTS

AUTHOR	HICKS, P.	CLASS 778.932
TITLE	Photographing butterflies and other insects	

Photographing
BUTTERFLIES
AND OTHER INSECTS

PHOTOGRAPHS AND TEXT BY

Paul Hicks

DESIGNED BY GRANT BRADFORD

FOUNTAIN PRESS

For Martine, Sean and Emma

Published by
FOUNTAIN PRESS LIMITED
Fountain House
2 Gladstone Road
Kingston-upon-Thames
Surrey KT1 3HD

Text and Photographs
PAUL HICKS

Series Designer
Grant Bradford

Layout
Alisa Tingley

Page Planning
Rex Carr

Text Editor
Graham Saxby

Index
Leigh Priest

Colour Origination
Global Colour Separation Ltd

Printed and Bound
in Hong Kong

ISBN 0 86343 332 4

CONTENTS

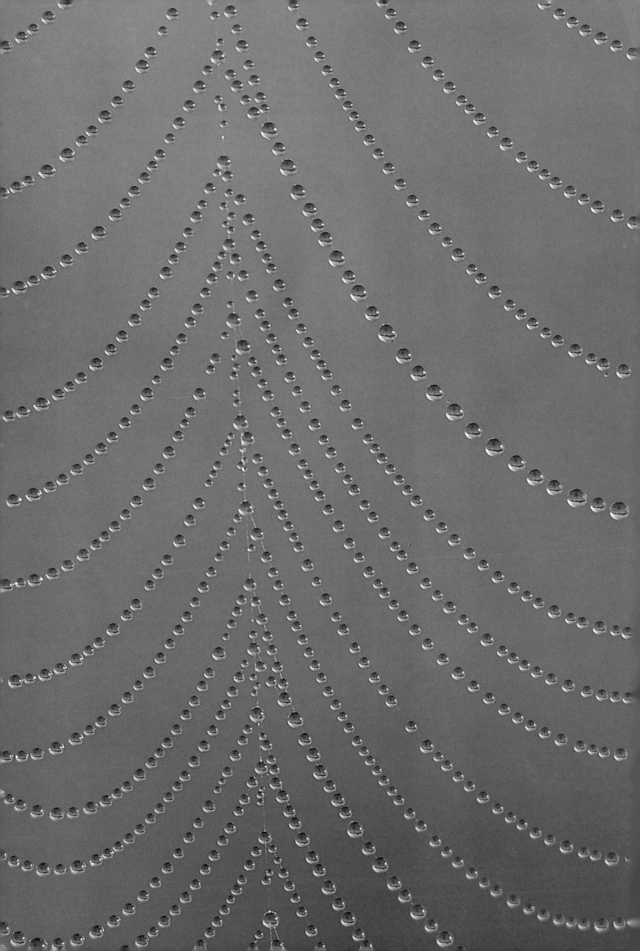

PREFACE

Photograph - Malcolm Freeman

Insects are ideal subjects for anyone with an interest in nature photography. They are abundant (at least during the warmer months), accessible, and wonderfully photogenic. There are no endurance tests in cramped hides as is so often the case with bird and mammal photography, and it is possible to get fine results with quite basic 35mm equipment.

This book outlines in detail the approach which I use to photograph insects and other invertebrates in the field, which may be a garden, a park, or, if you are fortunate enough to have access to the countryside, perhaps a flower-filled meadow.

Nearly all of my photography is done in the field because I feel that there is still plenty of scope in this area to shoot original pictures with some aesthetic appeal, particularly if you exploit the subtle qualities of natural light and make use of nature's own compositions. Studio photography doesn't really captivate me. Whilst the studio remains the only answer for photographers who need to shoot extreme-magnification close-ups or high-speed flash sequences of insect flight, I am content with less specialised work.

For me field photography has one other attraction, inasmuch as I love being out in the countryside with my camera, especially when I'm wading through a dewy meadow at first light in midsummer. This type of photography can be exacting but no one could seriously call it hard work.

Photographing insects is not just about recording rare species or unusual aspects of insect behaviour on film; you don't have to be a biologist with a camera. My aim is simply to produce pictures which are visually appealing, regardless of how common or rare the subject happens to be. At the same time, I'm careful to ensure my pictures remain authentic in terms of what they tell the viewer about nature. Exerting creative control when taking a picture means manipulating it to some extent. The challenge for the wildlife photographer lies in doing this without misrepresenting nature.

Whether you are new to insect photography or a more experienced hand not happy with your results so far, I hope that you will gain from using the same techniques used to shoot the illustrations in this book. Do pay attention to detail, because more than anything else it is sloppy technique that lets down unsuccessful photographers.

As nature photography grows in popularity so the potential increases for sensitive habitats to be damaged by careless photographers. Try not to become so intent on getting pictures that you unwittingly kneel on a precious plant or trample the eggs of a ground-nesting bird. Beware of the practice euphemistically known as gardening, i.e. cutting away vegetation in order to make the subject more obvious or to improve the background. As well as being destructive, this is unnecessary. Instead, you can tie back intrusive plants temporarily and leave them undamaged. If you stick to a set of self-imposed ethical guidelines you will enjoy your photography all the more for knowing you are doing no ecological harm.

Paul Hicks.

WINDSOR 1997

EQUIPMENT

Although medium and large format cameras are still favoured for such applications as portrait and landscape photography, the 35mm single-lens reflex (SLR) camera has come to dominate most other areas, including wildlife photography. Versatility, ease of use and compact size are the 35mm SLR's great virtues, and the image quality which you can obtain with 35mm film is now so good that this format is routinely used to illustrate magazine covers and fill double-page spreads. The better 35mm systems offer an excellent range of lenses and close-up accessories, which are more practical for field use than their bulkier medium-format equivalents. 35mm equipment is my first choice for photographing insects.

CHOOSING A CAMERA

There is now a bewildering range of cameras available, many of them marketed on their ability to 'think' for the photographer. Sophistication is everything, especially so in models aimed at the beginner. Market leaders such as Canon, Nikon and Minolta know that most people want to be able to take pictures without having to learn a lot of photographic theory, hence the rise of the autofocus, auto-everything camera that does it all for you. The profusion of automated features on these cameras obscures the reality, namely that their basic function is a simple one: a camera is basically just a light-tight box which exposes a piece of film to a measured amount of light for a measured amount of time. So what do you actually need on a camera for shooting insect close-ups?

AUTOFOCUS (AF)

This feature is standard on all but a handful of modern SLRs. AF technology is now extremely efficient and is constantly improving. Its main advantage is that in most situations it can focus faster than the photographer. With fast-action photography the best AF systems are also more accurate. They can track moving subjects and even allow for their movement during the brief delay which occurs between the photographer pressing the shutter release and the shutter actually firing.

Large White butterflies mating. 105mm macro lens, 1/4sec. at f/11.

The Achilles heel of most AF systems is that they will only focus on whatever is in the centre of the frame, so if you wish to focus on an off-centre subject, you must first place it centre-frame, then lock the focus, recompose and shoot. This doesn't represent much of an advance over focusing manually, and for close-up it is actually less precise.

The latest AF developments have gone some way to addressing this problem. A few cameras are now equipped with multiple AF sensors, spread across the frame so that the photographer can select whichever is closest to the desired point of focus. Canon's EOS 5 features a unique alternative, an infrared sensor monitoring the photographer's eye. The camera can tell what part of the frame you are looking at, and will focus on that area.

Having acknowledged the superiority of autofocus for certain applications, I still don't regard it as a great asset for close-up work. It is rarely necessary to be able to focus within milliseconds when photographing insects, as will become clearer when we get to the subject of technique. You should also bear in mind that not all of the major manufacturers offer a full range of compatible close-up accessories for their AF cameras. Nikon have an edge on their competitors in this respect, because all of their AF cameras to date incorporate a lens mount which remains compatible with their extensive range of manual focus lenses and accessories.

Although my cameras have AF, I invariably focus manually. By all means buy an autofocus camera (after all, you will probably use it for more than just photographing insects, in which case you might need the AF) but make sure that the lenses which are compatible with it can easily be focused manually when necessary.

MOTORISED FILM ADVANCE

A built-in autowind or motor drive is another feature that is now almost universal on modern SLRs, having largely replaced thumb-lever mechanisms for advancing the film. For the insect photographer, a motorised camera's ability to shoot continuous sequences of several frames per second is not a big advantage. Photographing insects with natural light requires a painstaking, methodical approach, with none of the fast-action, fast-shutter-speed shooting for which you would need a motor drive. Similarly, with flash close-ups you normally have to pause between shots to allow the flash to recharge. Nevertheless, motorised film

Sympetrum dragonfly.
180mm macro lens, with
52.5mm and 27.5mm extension
tubes, 1sec. at f/11.

advance is a useful feature. Sometimes it's helpful to be able to shoot at just the right instant, perhaps to capture some fleeting moment of behaviour or possibly to catch a brief lull in the wind when the subject is still; with a motorised camera there is less chance of the crucial moment occurring while you are busy winding on!

Another advantage with a motor wind is that it will not disturb the alignment of a tripod-mounted camera. In close-up photography the magnified image is very sensitive to disturbance. If you are using a manual film advance it is easy to unwittingly move the camera slightly as you wind on. Even a small nudge can noticeably affect your composition or focus, so you need to check for this before each shot.

There are still some cameras on the market which have manual film advance, although most of these will accept an add-on motor wind. These cameras tend to be mechanical rather than electronic and are favoured by photographers who value their reliability over the convenience of motorised models, which are (theoretically at least) more likely to malfunction and are entirely dependent on batteries.

PROGRAMMED EXPOSURE MODES

These lie at the heart of the electronic SLR's ability to 'think' for the photographer. Whereas manual cameras require the photographer to set the correct combination of lens aperture and shutter speed to ensure a well-exposed picture, a programmed camera takes care of this automatically. The most basic program modes simply select a combination of aperture and shutter speed which would be adequate for general photography. Such programs are unsuitable for more specialised work. For instance, the shutter speed will generally be too slow to freeze fast sports action, whilst the depth of field, or area of sharpness before and behind the point of focus, will probably be too shallow for close-up photography.

In an attempt to tailor programs to more specialised areas of photography, camera manufacturers have devised biased programs which produce certain effects. Many cameras now offer 'action' programs, 'portrait' programs, 'close-up' programs and so on. These attempt to simulate the exposure that a professional photographer might use in a given situation. These specialised programs will usually produce technically sound pictures, but they should not be regarded as a substitute for a proper understanding of exposure. You might benefit from using a multi-program camera to begin with, because nothing is more encouraging than initial success. However, if you are serious about your photography, sooner or later you will need a finer degree of control over your pictures than a program will allow. This is why I suggest that you opt for a camera which has a fully manual exposure mode in addition to any program modes it offers.

MULTIPLE METERING MODES

All current SLRs have a built-in light meter which measures the amount of light being reflected back from whatever is framed in the viewfinder. The camera's computer bases its exposure calculations on these readings, so their accuracy is critical. Unfortunately, reflected-light meters are easily confused by variations in the tone of different subjects, which they wrongly interpret as changes in the level of available light. Without some corrective input from the photographer, a substantial proportion of pictures end up being incorrectly exposed. In recent years, camera manufacturers have sought to develop a metering system intelligent enough to cope with subjects of almost any

Mating Gatekeeper butterflies. 105mm macro lens with 52.5mm extension tube, 1/250sec. at f/11 with flash.

tone, as well as with difficult lighting situations. The much-hyped 'evaluative' or 'matrix' metering system takes five or more readings from different areas of the picture and automatically compensates for excessively light or dark areas which would fool a more basic system.

If you are using the camera on a point-and-shoot basis in one of its program or auto-exposure modes, evaluative metering will produce a higher percentage of accurate exposures than any of the more basic metering modes. It can be very useful when photographing insects with a dedicated flash set-up, because it reduces the need to dial in exposure compensation.

For daylight photography, which normally allows a more methodical approach, I usually set the exposure manually, and for this I prefer either centre-weighted or spot metering. Spot metering tends to be confined to cameras designed for professional use. Both take a basic reading from an area in the middle of the frame; they differ mainly in the size of the area which they meter.

Of the two, I find spot metering particularly useful, because it takes a selective reading from a tiny area of the frame. If necessary you can use a spot meter to double-check your exposure by taking several readings from different parts of the picture before shooting.

In order to make best use of either form of metering you need some knowledge of the principles of exposure. A centre-weighted or spot meter will only give an accurate reading if it is directed at a true middletone, so if you meter something significantly lighter or darker, you must compensate accordingly when setting the exposure.

Bee in Lavatera flower.
105mm macro lens with 52.5mm extension tube, 1/250sec. at f/16 with flash.

DEPTH-OF-FIELD PREVIEW

This feature was once regarded as standard on any good camera, but it is omitted from the specification of many current SLRs. It is important to realise that when you are using the small lens apertures common in close-up photography, the image which appears on the film will differ considerably from the image which you see in the viewfinder. I am referring here to the depth of field, or the area of the picture that appears to be sharp in front of and behind the actual point of focus. This can be much deeper than it appears to be in the viewfinder, with the result that objects which appeared out of focus as you took the picture may be sharp in the photograph. A depth-of-field preview facility closes down the iris diaphragm and enables you to see the image as it will appear on film. This makes it an invaluable asset when selecting the correct aperture and it would be a key feature that I would look for.

REMOTE RELEASE SOCKET

When using a tripod-mounted camera, as you must when photographing insects with natural light, it is essential to use a remote shutter release so as to avoid the risk of camera shake from your finger blurring the picture. Amazingly, some cameras make no provision for either the traditional type of cable release or an electronic remote release. Make sure that yours does, because this is the only practical way of triggering the camera for long exposures.

FLASH FACILITIES

Any versatile outfit for photographing insects should include some flash equipment, although there is no need for the complex multiple flash set-ups often used for studio photography. My minimum requirements of a camera in terms of its flash capability are that its synchronous shutter speed should be reasonably fast, and that it should accept a dedicated TTL flash (see below).

The synchronous shutter speed of a camera ('synch speed' for short) is the fastest shutter speed which will synchronise with a flash unit. Some older cameras have a slow synch speed of around 1/60sec. This is likely to cause difficulties if you use flash in bright daylight with moving subjects. In these circumstances, the slower the shutter speed, the more likelihood there is of picking up two images on film. One is the flash image, which of course you want, while the other is a shadowy daylight 'ghost' image; this normally appears as a blur around the subject and often ruins the picture. This problem is unlikely to arise with current cameras which have a synch speed of between 1/125 and 1/300sec., too fast for the daylight image to register.

A 'dedicated' flashgun is one designed to operate with a specific camera. The term 'TTL' means through-the-lens metering, i.e. when the flash fires, the light meter in the camera body monitors the amount of light reflecting back from the subject, enabling the camera to automatically cut off the flash when it has supplied the correct amount required to ensure an accurate exposure. This means that you do not have to make any complex exposure calculations, nor are you restricted to shooting at one particular aperture. As with all automatic exposure systems, TTL flash is not infallible, but its ease of use for quick shooting with active insects makes it a great asset. Fortunately it is widely available on cameras from all the major manufacturers.

Burnet moths mating on scabious. *105mm macro lens with 52.5mm extension tube, 1/4sec. at f/11*

Don't pay too much attention to the small pop-up flashes which are built in to many SLRs. If you are shooting insect close-ups, the flash needs to be mounted close to the front of the lens, ideally on a purpose-made bracket.

In conclusion: given the generous specification of most current SLRs, you are unlikely to have much trouble finding one which will cope with insect photography. However, you should look for three essential features which are sometimes omitted on many otherwise excellent cameras. These are:

- full manual exposure control
- depth-of-field preview
- remote release socket

I am reluctant to recommend particular cameras, partly because a comparison of different models could fill a book on its own, and partly because choosing a camera is largely down to personal preference in terms of the way it fits your hand and the feel of its controls. I like heavy, solid cameras which have traditional controls, i.e., knobs on the top! My choice is the Nikon F4S. You may prefer the control wheel systems, pushbuttons and LCD panels common to most other electronic SLRs.

Above left–
This damselfly was photographed with a 50mm lens. Because of the comparatively wide angle of view at this focal length, it was impossible to prevent the distracting strip of sky from intruding into the top of the frame. The 50mm also forced me to work too close to the subject - about 12cm away. *50mm lens with 14mm extension tube, 1sec. at f/11.*

Above right–
The whole exercise was much easier with a 180mm lens, its narrow field of view made it easy to exclude the sky, producing a cleaner background, and the extra focal length provided much more working distance; the damselfly posed happily while I shot from about 40cm away. *180mm macro lens, 1sec. at f/11.*

The build quality of the leading brands is broadly similar within a given price bracket, although some names seem to carry more kudos than others. In distinguishing between brands I would suggest that you look at the range of lenses and accessories which they offer. In this respect certain manufacturers score over others.

LENSES

Your choice of lens is possibly more important than your choice of camera, if only because the quality of the image which appears on film is ultimately limited by the quality of the lens. Of course, you must also use good technique, but a poor lens will always hinder you no matter how much care you take. Similarly, a lens of the wrong focal length will turn a field trip into an exercise in frustration. Too short, and it will force you to work too close to the subject. Too long, and it will not focus close enough, and your subjects will be too small in the frame.

CONVENTIONAL LENSES

Meadow brown and dew.
300mm IF-ED lens with 52.5mm and 27.5mm extension tubes, 1/4sec. at f/11.

Although macro lenses are considered ideal for close-up photography, it is possible to get excellent results with conventional lenses. Their obvious drawback, namely an inability to focus close enough, is easily overcome by using them in conjunction with extension tubes and/or supplementary close-up lenses. This is good news for anyone whose budget will not accommodate the outsize price tag of a macro lens, or who simply wishes to adapt an existing outfit for close-up work. A good conventional lens will produce very high quality close-ups, particularly if you just use extension tubes to make it focus closer. Such a combination will virtually match a macro lens in terms of the sharpness visible in a projected slide or a print.

This is not to say that conventional lenses will match macros in every respect. For one thing, they still fall short of macro lenses as regards the magnification you can obtain. For instance, a conventional 100mm lens fitted with a 50mm extension tube will provide only half the magnification you could expect one of the latest 100mm macros to yield on its own. The conventional lens can certainly be used to shoot a wide range of subjects, but it is not as versatile as the macro lens. Nor is it quite as convenient to use, as you always need to employ various combinations of accessories with it.

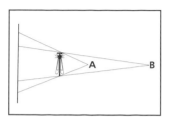

A comparison of the angles of view, working distances and background coverage obtained with 50mm lens (A) and 180mm lens (B).

MACRO LENSES

The term 'macro' is much abused by some lens manufacturers, who apply it to any lens – zooms and super-telephotos included – that will focus a little closer than average. Many of these lenses will not produce the image magnification which the term 'macro' implies, and their optical quality is usually unimpressive. Genuine macro lenses are invariably prime lenses, i.e., not zooms. They tend to fall into one of three categories of approximate focal length: 50 to 60mm, 90 to 105mm, and 180 or 200mm. They are designed primarily for close-up photography and therefore have an exceptional close-focusing capability. Without any added accessories, most of the newer macro lenses can produce a life-size image on the film, allowing the photographer to fill the frame with a large bumblebee or a small butterfly. Even greater magnifications are possible if you add accessories such as extension tubes, teleconverters or supplementary close-up lenses; you can then shoot extreme close-ups which will reveal the detail in compound eyes or the scales on a butterfly's wing.

Macro lenses also differ from conventional lenses in their optical design, which is corrected to produce extremely sharp and accurate close-up images. The benefits of this correction are most apparent when a macro lens is used for copying work, i.e. photographing documents or pictures. With a three-dimensional subject such as an insect, the optical superiority of a macro over a conventional lens is less evident. Nevertheless, if you use a macro lens you can be confident that it will give you the ultimate in close-up image quality.

FOCAL LENGTH

When photographers refer to lenses they identify them primarily by focal length, because this is the factor which most influences the look of the pictures they take. It also determines their suitability for various purposes. The range of lenses available for 35mm cameras is enormous, with focal lengths from 6mm to 2000mm. The 50mm 'standard' lens is generally reckoned to produce pictures which most closely resemble the human eye's view of the world. Pictures taken with shorter focal length, or 'wide-angle' lenses, take in a wider field of view than we are used to seeing, thus enhancing the steepness of perspective, so that a near object appears large in relation to the

Marbled white on rosebay willowherb.
200mm lens with 52.5mm extension tube, 1/8sec. at f/8.

background. Longer focal lengths, or telephotos, have a narrower field of view. This enables you to fill the frame with smaller or more distant subjects, and because the narrow field of view isolates a small part of a scene, part of the normal impression of perspective is lost. It is often said that wide-angle lenses exaggerate perspective, whilst telephotos compress it, neither statement being strictly true. Perspective is only altered by a change in viewpoint, not by the focal length of a lens.

While on the subject of photographic mythology, I should also mention that focal length has no bearing on depth of field. This is determined solely by the lens aperture and the image magnification. Don't be misled by anyone who tells you that you will get more depth of field if you use a shorter lens.

Focal length is the most important factor to consider when choosing a lens for photographing insects, especially where field work is concerned. This is mainly because it dictates how close to the subject you must be before it is large enough in the frame. Remember that you will frequently be trying to photograph flighty insects which will not allow a very close approach, and even with a tolerant subject other difficulties arise if a short lens forces you to work too close. Getting a tripod-mounted outfit into position is much more difficult. There is a constant danger of knocking the subject with your hand or a stray tripod leg, and the wider background coverage of the short lens tends to pick up distracting details that can spoil the shot.

Given these considerations, you might think a lens of 300mm or more would be ideal, but the drawback with really long focal lengths is that even when used with extension tubes, very few will focus close enough to produce enough image magnification. They also tend to have large filter threads, which may prevent you from using supplementary close-up lenses.

The answer is to find a compromise. If you are considering a conventional lens I would suggest something around the 100 to 135mm mark. This gives you a useful amount of working distance between lens and subject, and the amount of extension necessary to make it focus close enough will not prove impractical; a 50mm tube will bring a lot of subjects within your reach, and you will have no trouble finding compatible supplementary lenses. If you are considering macro lenses, a 100 or 105mm is still an excellent choice, but given that you will not be relying on accessories to obtain enough magnification, you could opt

Comma. Although long telephoto lenses do not make versatile tools for close-up photography, their great reach can make them very useful in certain situations. I came across this Comma basking among the leaf litter of an oak wood in April. Because it had been well warmed by the sun, it was too lively to allow a close approach with a 100 or 200mm lens. I photographed it from 1.5m away using a 300mm lens mounted on extension tubes. 300mm IF-ED lens with 52.5mm and 27.5mm extension tubes, 1/4sec. at f/11.

for a 180 or 200mm. The Canon EOS system now includes a 180mm f/3.5 macro, whilst Nikon offer an AF 200mm f/4. Both of these lenses focus to life-size. Two other 200mm f/4 macro lenses are available, these being a manual focus Canon FD lens which focuses to life-size, and the Nikon manual focus model which reaches half life-size. The FD lens is now discontinued and has become a highly sought-after secondhand item. A friend of mine advertised his recently and was almost trampled in the rush!

The main advantage with long macro lenses is that you get enough magnification along with the luxury of plenty of working distance. They also have a very narrow field of view, making it easy to exclude distracting background details when necessary. I regard these long macros as the ultimate lenses for field photography, but be warned, they are very expensive!

If your existing system happens to be neither Canon nor Nikon, or if you want a long macro lens for rather less money, an alternative is offered by Sigma, their 180mm APO-macro. Two variants are available, both of which focus to half life-size; the less expensive of the two has a maximum aperture of f/5.6, whilst the other offers an exceptional f/2.8. Although it is rarely desirable to actually

shoot at f/2.8 when photographing insects, this fast maximum aperture gives a very bright viewfinder image and is a great aid to precise focusing.

Hoverfly in poppy.
105mm macro lens with 52.5mm extension tube, 1/250sec. at f/16 with flash.

ZOOM LENSES

Although a zoom lens would not be my first choice for close-up work, it is possible to obtain excellent results if you use one in conjunction with extension tubes and/or supplementary lenses.

When using a zoom lens with extension tubes you will find that the image will no longer remain in focus as you zoom, so you will have to re-focus after reaching the desired focal length setting. You will also find that if you have zoomed towards the long end of its range, the subject won't necessarily be bigger in the frame as you would expect - in fact it will probably end up smaller. This is because the effect of any given length of added extension diminishes as focal length increases. The result is that as you zoom, the image magnification actually decreases. The only way to maintain or increase it is to add still more extension. Using a zoom on extension can get rather confusing!

Honeybee on mallow flower.
105mm macro lens with
27.5mm extension tube,
1/250sec. at f/16 with flash.

Life is more straightforward when using zoom lenses with supplementary close-up lenses, in which case the image remains in focus as you zoom, and – miraculously – as you zoom towards the long end of the lens's range, the size of the image increases dramatically, offering you a wide range of magnifications without the need to move closer to or further from the subject. Probably the ideal lens to use in this way is an 80-200, 70-210mm or even a 75-300mm provided that it has the correct size of filter thread.

LENS QUALITY

Whether you opt for a macro or a conventional lens, you should buy the best quality that you can afford. While there is little to choose between the various camera manufacturers in terms of the quality of their lenses (which is generally superb), more variation exists in the quality of lenses offered by the numerous independent lens manufacturers. The leading brands in this area, notably Sigma, Tamron and Tokina, now produce some really excellent optics, but there are still a few turkeys lurking at the bottom end of the market. Avoid cheap lenses from obscure manufacturers.

TRIPODS

Unless you intend to do all of your insect photography with flash, which would be a pity, you will need a good tripod. Without one it is impossible to shoot consistently sharp close-ups with natural light, because you will routinely have to use slow shutter speeds of 1/30sec. or less. With such slow exposures, camera shake will blur the picture if you try to hand-hold, and it will be particularly acute in the case of close-ups shot with 100 to 200mm lenses, which magnify camera shake as effectively as they magnify images! Nevertheless, many photographers try to get by without a tripod, perhaps because they feel it is too much trouble to carry one around and keep setting it up. Invariably when they compare their pictures with those they see published in magazines and books, they put the difference in sharpness down to the lenses used, as if simply owning an expensive lens makes razor-sharp results a foregone conclusion.

In fact, the best way to guarantee sharp results is to use a tripod habitually, so you need to get used to the idea that photographing an insect without flash is not a matter of raising the camera to the eye, clicking away a couple of times and moving on. Sometimes you may need to spend half an hour or more on shooting a few good portraits of a roosting butterfly. Be prepared to spend enough to get a good tripod. Although there are very few really poor cameras and lenses around, most camera shops are well stocked with badly designed tripods.

My first requirement of a tripod is stability. Its legs should not bend even when fully extended, and it should be heavy. A lightweight tripod may seem steady when it is standing on the floor of the shop, but once it is set up among tussocks of long grass it will just totter about hopelessly. Don't be swayed by assurances that you can always hang your camera bag underneath it; sometimes you'll need to set it up just above the ground.

The tripod's ability to support the camera close to ground level would be my next consideration, because this is where you will find many of your subjects. The need to get down low immediately rules out conventional designs with cross-bracing between the legs and centre column. With these, it is not possible to get the camera much less than about two feet off the ground, except by fitting it upside down to the bottom end of the centre column. Because I believe in keeping field outfits as convenient as possible

The Benbo tripod is versatile and very sturdy.
In my opinion, the centre column as supplied is too long; it must be tilted if you wish to support the camera close to ground level, so that a three-way pan/tilt head no longer functions in the normal way. By shortening the centre column it can remain upright whilst supporting the camera less than 30cm above the ground.

Small Heath butterfly.
Macro lenses are not
essential for photographing
insects. This shot was taken
with a conventional 200mm
lens mounted on an
extension tube and fitted
with an inexpensive
supplementary close-up lens.
200mm lens, 52.5mm extension
tube, Nikon 3T supplementary,
1/2sec. at f/11.

to use, I would not put up with having to work with a camera that is suspended upside down in the awkward space between three tripod legs. Go for a tripod which has no cross-bracing, but has a positive mechanism to lock the legs in position when they are fully opened out. The tripod should not sink an inch or so before the locking mechanism engages properly, nor should it gradually give under the weight of the camera, regardless of how low it is set up.

Long centre columns are another handicap when you need to get the camera down low. With some designs, you can tilt the centre column so it is almost parallel to the ground, but even if this is possible it makes a normal pan/tilt tripod head awkward to use, for as you pan and tilt the camera, the vertical and horizontal controls are wildly off-axis and this can make framing a shot frustrating.

There are two solutions to the problem of long centre columns. One is to buy a short replacement centre column if one is available from the manufacturer. Failing that, you can cut the existing one down with a hacksaw, even though this might bring a tear to your eye if the tripod is brand new!

It is important that the tripod should support the camera at eye level, preferably without the centre column being extended. In any sort of photography it is irritating to have to stoop to see through the viewfinder when you could otherwise stand upright. With insect close-ups, too short a tripod will also prevent you from aligning the camera properly on subjects which you find higher up in bushes or on tree trunks.

Finally I would check the tripod's legs, particularly the locks on the joints between sections. As well as being positive, they should not be vulnerable to clogging by dirt and grit.

Only a handful of tripods are really well suited to photographing insects in field conditions. These include a couple of professional models from Manfrotto and Slik. Two other makes are favoured by nature photographers, namely Gitzo and Benbo. Gitzo tripods have a fairly conventional design but can be set up very low, and it is possible to obtain short centre columns. They are extremely well made, and rock solid at any height, although they are correspondingly expensive.

Benbo tripods, my own choice, have a unique design whereby all three legs are locked by a single lever, and like Gitzos they are very versatile, and genuinely designed for field use. The Benbo's centre column is rather long, and

Dark Green Fritillary.
These butterflies are very
nervous during the brief
spells when they are not on
the wing, and I knew that
any attempt to get in close to
this one would send it
fluttering away on the
breeze. I opted for a 300mm
lens and was able to shoot
from about 1.5m away.
300mm IF-ED lens with 52.5mm
and 27.5mm extension tubes,
1/60sec. at f/5.6.

mine fell victim to the hacksaw long ago. Be warned that unless you are less than about 5 ft tall, cutting off the centre column of a Benbo Mk1 will prevent it from supporting the camera at eye level, so it's better to butcher the longer-legged Mk2.

TRIPOD HEADS

Your tripod will not be complete without a tripod head. Most good tripods are sold headless, on the assumption that the photographer will wish to fit whatever pattern most suits his or her needs. There are several basic types of design, the simplest being the ball-and-socket head, which when unlocked frees the camera to move in any direction. Despite the simplicity of the design, don't expect a good one to be cheap. You will need a well-made model that is capable of locking a heavy outfit solidly in position.

Another type of head is the three-way pan/tilt, in which the horizontal/vertical/rotational movement of the camera can be controlled separately. Whilst some photographers like the quick adjustment of ball-and-socket heads, I prefer a three-way pan-tilt because I think its ability to lock different planes of movement independently encourages careful composition. Instead of trying to concentrate on everything at once, you are able to lock up two of the three control handles and compose the shot one step at a time. For example, you can pan so as to move the subject a little to one side without disturbing a level horizon. As with ball-and-socket designs, it is important to choose a well-made head which allows smooth movement of the camera but which locks solid, so avoid anything that is made largely of plastics. Another thing to watch out for is a pet hate of mine, an abnormally long control handle, half a metre long in some cases. When you are shooting insect close-ups with the camera set up in awkward positions, it will either catch in your clothing or poke you in the chest while you are trying to focus.

If you do all your insect photography with a lens that has a built in tripod collar, there is another type of head which you could consider. This is the fluid video head. Although these are designed for video cameras, their fluid-damped pan/tilt action is a joy to use when composing magnified close-ups. Unfortunately they generally lack any provision for rotating the camera off the horizontal, which is why you can only use them with lenses that have tripod collars.

Don't feel restricted to choosing a tripod head from your tripod's manufacturer. They all have standard $^3/_8$ or $^1/_4$ in. screw threads, so the various makes are all compatible.

OTHER FIELD ACCESSORIES

FLASH UNITS

A flash unit Is really a must, because it frees you to hand-hold the camera and shoot insects which are too active to capture with slow natural-light exposures and tripod-mounted equipment. My preference for this type of work is a small conventional flash unit mounted on a home-made bracket so as to sit just above the front of the lens. This gives a surprisingly natural-looking form of lighting, quite unlike the harsh shadowy effect you might expect after having used small single flashes for more conventional photography.

As far as the specification of the flash is concerned, my main requirement would be that it should be a genuine TTL unit, because TTL metering makes life so much easier when you are trying to shoot quickly in the field.

Don't confuse automatic flash with the dedicated TTL system. Unlike the latter, an automatic unit is not controlled by the camera; the flash regulates its own output by means of a small forward-facing light meter. This works reasonably well for general photography, but it is nowhere near as efficient as the TTL system, especially for close-up work, when the flash may meter the wrong area. The chances are that you will have to opt for a TTL flash from your camera's manufacturer. Of the independent brands which are available I have yet to see any which are

small and light enough to mount on a bracket for insect close-ups. The smaller a unit is, the better, because it will be easier to handle and less likely to put a wary subject to flight as you move in to shoot. You also want a short recycling time. There is nothing worse than missing a good shot because your subject flew away while you were waiting for the flash to recharge.

A ring flash is another option. These specialised flashes were originally designed for medical photography and fit around the front of the lens, providing very flat, shadowless illumination. To my eyes, this sort of lighting looks very unnatural in insect close-ups, and it surprises me that ring flashes are so widely recommended for this purpose. Some units do offer the facility to switch off part of the ring, in which case you get the same effect as with the much less expensive bracket-mounted flash unit.

EXTENSION TUBES

One of the best ways to make a lens focus closer is to fit an extension tube between the lens and the camera. As the name suggests, an extension tube is little more than a hollow metal tube. It contains no glass, and does not magnify the image or affect the focal length of the lens. It works in accordance with optical laws which dictate that when a lens is moved further away from the film plane in the camera, the point of focus is brought closer. With most lenses this principle is evident when you turn the focusing ring towards its minimum focus setting; as you do so, the lens appears to increase in length. In fact, what you see is the whole optical assembly being moved outward. An extension tube is simply a means of extending this process beyond its normal limit.

Extension tubes are available in various lengths. Nikon for instance offer the following: 8mm, 14mm, 27.5mm and 52.5mm. Of these, the latter two are the most useful, and you can use them either singly or together to adapt a conventional lens for close-ups. They can also be used to improve the versatility of a macro lens.

An alternative way of adding extension is to use a bellows unit, but I feel that these have disadvantages as far as field photography is concerned. They are cumbersome, and because they are primarily designed for high magnification studio close-ups, they generally do not allow you to use small amounts of extension should you wish to do so. Some of them also lack automatic metering linkages, which

Common Blue basking.
I wanted to photograph this exquisite male common blue using natural light, because it is the morning sun glistening on its wings that really makes the shot.
Other blues were already on the wing, and I knew that this one could probably fly were I to disturb him.
My biggest problem was getting the tripod into position, but after making a very slow, careful approach and avoiding sudden movements as I framed him and focused, I got four frames before he flew off. All of them were pin sharp and identically composed, thanks to the tripod.
105mm macro lens with 14mm extension tube, 1/30sec. at f/11.

A typical set-up for shooting daylight exposures of insects. The tripod has been set at low level to align the camera on a small butterfly. With the sun still below the horizon I am using a reflector to bounce as much light as possible on to the subject. My shirt has been laid on the long grass in the immediate background to flatten it and prevent it from encroaching into the shot. The exposure time is likely to be as long as 2secs., so the camera will be triggered by a remote release.

makes estimating and setting the exposure a lengthier process. They are also more expensive and less robust than extension tubes.

Extension tubes do have disadvantages. Any form of extension will reduce the amount of light reaching the film, and so compel you to shoot at slower shutter speeds. Also, the effect of any given amount of extension diminishes as focal length increases. The longer the lens, the more extension it will need to produce a particular magnification, to the extent that the amount of extension needed to make a conventional 200mm lens focus to life-size would prove impractical for field use.

SUPPLEMENTARY CLOSE-UP LENSES

These lenses screw on to the front of the lens in the same way as filters, which they closely resemble. They enable a conventional lens to focus closer so as to produce worthwhile close-up magnifications, and they can be used to increase the maximum magnification of a macro lens.

Two varieties of supplementary lens are available, and these differ significantly in their performance. The more common single-element type significantly degrades the image quality, especially at large apertures. The two-element type is more fully corrected, and its quality is excellent. Examples of this type are the Nikon 3T and 4T, which fit 52mm filter threads, and the Nikon 5T and 6T which are a 62mm fit. Canon offer the 250D with 52mm or 58mm threads (recommended for focal lengths between 38 and 135mm) and the 500D with 52mm, 58mm, 72mm and

Common Blue damselfly on
seedhead. *180mm macro lens*
with 52.5mm extension tube,
1/4sec. at f/8.

77mm threads (recommended for focal lengths between 75 and 300mm). All of these can be used with any make of lens, provided it has the appropriate filter thread.

Supplementaries come in various strengths, measured in 'dioptres'. They are commonly available in strengths of between 1 and 3 dioptres. Like any lens, a supplementary lens has a particular focal length, and this can be determined by dividing 1000mm by its strength in dioptres. Thus a +1 dioptre supplementary has a focal length of 1000mm, a +2 is 500mm, a +3 is 333mm and so on. Knowing the focal length of a supplementary will in turn tell you what image magnification it will yield when combined with a particular prime lens. Just divide the focal length of the prime lens by that of the supplementary. For instance, if you mount a +2 dioptre supplementary (which has a focal length of 500mm) on a 100mm lens, you will get a magnification of 1:5 (or one-fifth life-size) on the film.

Supplementaries are unique among close-up accessories in that they enable a lens to focus closer without causing any reduction in the amount of light reaching the film. This alone can make them a great asset, and they are less expensive than some of the longer extension tubes or teleconvertors. A further advantage with supplementaries is that they provide larger magnifications with longer lenses than they do with short ones. If you own a longer lens and have been struggling to make it focus close enough by adding large amounts of extension, a supplementary could be the solution. Alternatively, you may have run into problems using a zoom on extension, which can be rather awkward; again, a supplementary could be the answer.

Of course, there has to be a drawback to using supplementaries, and this is that they reduce the focal length of the prime lens. This effect varies according to the strength of the supplementary and the focal length of the prime lens. For instance the +3 dioptre Nikon 4T would reduce a 100mm lens to about 80mm - not a very significant loss. However, a proportionately greater reduction occurs with longer lenses; the 4T would turn a 200mm into a 125mm, so you pay for the extra magnification by losing a lot of working distance.

TELECONVERTERS

Like an extension tube, a teleconverter (also known as an extender or multiplier) fits between the camera and lens. Here the similarity ends, because a teleconverter contains glass elements and works by increasing the focal length of the lens, thus magnifying the image. It does not affect the minimum focus distance of the lens.

Teleconverters are commonly available in two strengths, X1.4 and X2. These are the factors by which they multiply the focal length, so a X1.4 converter would turn a 100mm lens into a 140mm. On its own, neither the X1.4 nor the X2 would be sufficient to transform a conventional lens into a useful close-up lens; you would still have to use them in conjunction with extension tubes. However, when used in this way, or when combined with a macro lens, either one would give you more magnification and/or more working distance, which is an important consideration.

The biggest drawback with teleconverters is that they reduce the amount of light reaching the film. In the case of the X1.4, you lose one stop, which means that if you set the lens aperture to say, f/11, you would be shooting at f/16. The X2 costs you two stops, enough to be a real hindrance at times, because it reduces the shutter speed, dims the viewfinder and makes precise focusing more difficult.

There is some loss of image quality when a converter is fitted, although with care this effect can be minimised. It is least pronounced when shooting with smaller lens apertures (which is the norm in close-up photography anyway) and is less evident with X1.4 than X2 converters. It also depends on the quality of the converter. As with any lens, use the best you can afford.

If you already own a teleconverter it can certainly be put to good use, but acquiring one would not be among my first priorities when putting together a close-up outfit. Good

Above left–
Ichneumon fly. In order to get an unobstructed view of the fly, I had to shoot from such an angle that it was thrown into shadow by the first rays of the sun.
Thus much of the colour and detail of the subject is lost.
105mm macro lens with 27.5mm extension tube, 1/15sec. at f/8

Above right–
The shot is transformed by the use of a reflector, which has directed a little sunlight on to the fly so as to highlight it against the background.
105mm macro lens, 52.5mm extension tube, 1/15sec. at f/8.

Teleconverters are as expensive as good prime lenses, and on their own they are not useful enough to justify the expense. If you do buy one, ensure that it is compatible with your lens. Some converters are designed for certain focal lengths, and cannot be fitted to other lenses, even though they may be from the same manufacturer.

FOCUSING RAILS

I would suggest that when you begin photographing insects you should not attempt to shoot at very large magnifications, because all of the normal difficulties associated with close-up photography become more acute as magnification increases. However, as your technique improves you will no doubt become more ambitious. Once you do start to shoot beyond life-size, the positioning of the camera becomes critical, a centimetre or so either way making a significant difference to the size of the image.

A focusing rail is the ideal solution to the problem of having to manoeuvre a hefty tripod-mounted outfit into precise position. It is basically an adjustable platform which fits between the camera and the tripod head, and it enables you to make fine adjustments without moving the

Small Tortoiseshell in wheat field. A remote release is essential when you are using a tripod-mounted outfit for natural light exposures, in order to eliminate the risk of camera shake from your fingers blurring the picture. This is particularly true when shooting at high magnifications or when using long lenses, which are very sensitive to vibration. For this shot, I needed the working distance of a 300mm to avoid disturbing the butterfly.
300mm IF-ED lens with 52.5mm and 27.5mm extension tubes, 1/15sec. at f/8.

tripod. As with most field accessories, the more compact it is, the more practical it is to carry and use. I have a small and inexpensive Pentax MkIII which I find ideal.

REFLECTORS & DIFFUSERS

These are the means by which you can control the effect of natural light in your pictures. A reflector normally consists of a flat disc with a stippled silver finish. Commercial patterns have a collapsible frame and fold down for easier storage, although I get by with a more improvised design, namely silver cardboard cakestands which slot neatly into my camera bag. Reflectors are used to bounce light on to areas of the shot which need to be better lit, usually the subject itself. If the light is falling on the subject from the wrong angle a reflector is usually the best solution, and

I use one in preference to fill-in flash, which rarely looks as natural.

A diffuser generally consists of a piece of translucent white gauze stretched over a rigid frame, and it is used to soften direct sunlight, which is normally too harsh and tends to produce very contrasty pictures with unsightly dark shadows. By placing a diffuser between the subject and the sun, highlights are toned down and shadows are less obvious. The whole effect is much more pleasing in an insect portrait.

Reflectors and diffusers can also serve as makeshift windbreaks. One of the constant problems when photographing insects clinging to frail plant stems is wind movement. If there is any real wind blowing you may find it impossible to shoot longish daylight exposures, but the effects of a light breeze can often be overcome by shielding the subject with your reflector.

GREY CARD

This is an often neglected accessory which can prove invaluable when you are shooting manual exposures with natural light. The function of a grey card is to provide the photographer with a reliable reference from which to take a reflected-light reading. Its reflectance is precisely 18%, the same tone that is used to calibrate the camera's meter. Provided you place the grey card in the same light as the subject, a meter reading taken from it will ensure a correctly exposed photograph.

FILTERS

A filter is used to change (and preferably enhance) some aspect of the photograph. Filters can broadly be divided into two types. Glass filters screw directly into the filter thread in the front of the lens, whilst gelatin and plastic filters slot into a holder; this is usually left on the lens so that different filters can be changed as required. I prefer glass filters, as these are less easily scratched and do not require the careful handling and storage essential with the more vulnerable gelatin types.

I use only two varieties of filter. One is a circular polarizer, which cuts down the glare from reflective surfaces such as shiny leaves or water, and gives their underlying colour more punch on film. Unfortunately a polarizer's usefulness is often restricted as, when used to full effect, it robs you of two stops of precious light.

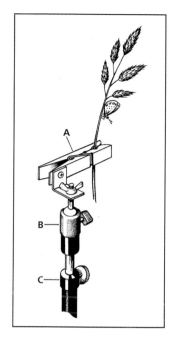

Home-made 'third arm' used to steady a frail perch. This useful accessory consists of: (A) Clothes peg, with padded jaws; (B) Small ball-and-socket tripod head; (C) Angler's telescopic bank stick. The tripod head is screwed onto the bank stick via a commercially-made adaptor; these are available from mail-order fishing tackle suppliers.

This mayfly's legs and the tracery of veins on its wings would have been lost against a busy background. The 180mm lens, with its narrow angle of view, has excluded distracting elements in the background. The result is a very clean and simple shot which emphasises the frailty of the subject. 180mm macro lens, 1/4sec. at f/8.

The other filter which sometimes comes in handy is an 81 series 'warming' filter. This can be used to counteract the slight bluish tint which may appear on film under overcast conditions, or when shooting a shaded subject under a blue sky. The 81A is the most subtle of the series.

Because I strive to retain a natural feel to my pictures, I don't use special effects filters. These can add sparkle to pinpoints of light, surround subjects with a supposedly romantic haze, or even change the colour of the sky from say, an overcast grey to blue or sunset orange. In my opinion, photographic cliches of this sort are best avoided. When I see nature photographs overlaid with gimmicky filter effects it is as if the photographer is saying, 'the picture wasn't interesting enough, so I used a filter'. Other photographers see things differently and regard filters as a means of being more creative, so it would be wrong to suggest that everyone should share my attitude. All I will say is, don't rely on filters to improve a poor picture. Look for a better picture!

A THIRD ARM

Not the anatomical peculiarity that it may sound, but a means of combating wind movement, the ever-present enemy when you are shooting long daylight exposures of insects clinging to frail grass stems and other vegetation. Although some specialist retailers supply commercially-made versions of the third arm, mine is home-made. It consists of an angler's telescopic bank stick – basically a pointed aluminium pole, 50-100cm long – fitted with a small ball-and-socket tripod head. (This screws in to the bank stick's 3/8in. thread via a purpose-made adaptor). Fixed to the tripod head is a plastic clothes peg with jaws padded with pieces of foam draught-excluder strip. The bank stick is pushed into the ground next to the subject's perch, and the peg is then carefully clamped around the stem just out of shot, so as to steady it. The foam padding will protect most plant stems from damage, but some common sense is obviously required in order to avoid damaging anything particularly fragile. It certainly should not be used on orchids or other precious plants.

Although the third arm is impractical for use with active insects, it will prove invaluable if you do much natural-light work with static subjects such as roosting butterflies, particularly if you use it in conjunction with a windbreak.

A BASIC OUTFIT

Given the array of close-up accessories described so far, you could be forgiven for thinking that you will end up clanking off into the undergrowth laden down with a backbreaking collection of ironmongery. In fact, a very versatile field outfit can be built around a few key items of equipment; I would recommend that you start with the following–

- camera body
- prime lens of between 100 and 135mm with
  25mm and 50mm (approx) extension tubes,
    or a macro lens of approx 100 or 200mm
- sturdy tripod with 3-way pan/tilt head
- cable release or electronic remote release
- small TTL flash unit and short TTL cord
- grey card
- flash bracket ⎤
- reflector   ⎟
                ⎬—— can be home-made
- diffuser   ⎟
- third arm   ⎦

This outfit would enable you to photograph insects at magnifications up to life-size (1:1), using natural light or flash. Only quite specialised work involving extreme magnifications or high-speed flash shots of flying insects would be beyond its capabilities.

FILM

PRINT FILM VS. TRANSPARENCY

All of my nature photography is shot on transparency (slide) film. This is mainly because transparencies are preferred by magazine and book publishers, but there are other reasons why I would not normally use print film. First, while prints may be more convenient to view, I feel that nothing really compares with a projected transparency. If you want prints, you can have them done from transparencies anyway. Secondly, pictures shot on transparency film give you an exact representation of the exposure which you set when you took the picture. A common complaint among photographers who use print film and send it to commercial labs is that all the exposures look the same, despite the fact that they bracketed or deliberately under- or over-exposed to achieve certain effects. This is because the variations in exposure are

Painted Lady on buddleia.
105mm macro lens,
1/60sec. at f/8.

automatically compensated for during the printing process: like cameras, printing machines assume that every picture should be middle-toned. This is a bit tough if you've filled the frame with a white butterfly, because the machine will do its best to make it mid-grey! The best way around this problem is to do your own printing. Failing that, you must pay big money for hand printing at the lab, or suffer untold frustration every time their machine interprets your creativity as incompetence, and 'corrects' your 'mistakes'.

With transparencies, no such problems arise. There is no printing stage involved, so as far as the exposure is concerned, what you set is what you get. Of course, you have no safety net should you make a mistake, so using transparency film soon teaches you to expose accurately.

FILM SPEED

35mm film is widely available in speeds ranging from ISO25 to ISO1600. These ISO numbers offer a guide to the speed with which a particular film responds to light. At any given light level and lens aperture, the faster the film, the faster the shutter speed you will be able to use. Although it is usually an advantage to be able to use fast shutter speeds (which make camera shake and subject movement less likely to blur the picture), fast films are 'grainier' than their slow counterparts. As a result, they cannot match the razor-sharp quality of slow films.

All of my insect photography is done with slow film, because my preference is for extremely sharp, virtually grain-free pictures. When using natural light, this means accepting the limitations which longer exposures impose. You can eliminate camera shake by using a tripod, but there is not much you can do with an active subject or excessive wind movement, short of resorting to flash.

Any film with an ISO number of less than 100 would generally be regarded as slow. For many years Kodak dominated among slower films with Kodachrome 25 and 64, but in recent years Fuji have made a big impact with Velvia. Although Velvia purports to be an ISO50 film, most photographers rate it one-third of a stop slower at ISO40. It therefore falls mid-way between the two Kodachromes in terms of speed. Kodak's response to the success of Velvia has been to introduce a similar ISO50 film of their own, Ektachrome Panther 50. All four of these films give extremely sharp results.

The fastest films I would consider using for insect close-ups would be Kodak's Ektachrome Panther 100 and Fuji Sensia 100 (or its professional equivalent, Provia). These are exceptionally sharp for their rated speed of ISO 100.

FILM COMPARISON

Different films vary considerably in terms of the way they reproduce colour, and in their processing requirements. Kodachrome films are notably sharp, but by comparison with Velvia their colour rendition looks rather muted. Velvia is renowned for reproducing extremely punchy, saturated colours, which is one reason it has met with such success. Another reason is that whereas the Kodachrome has to be returned to Kodak for processing, Velvia is an E-6 process film, so it can be processed by any commercial lab. Kodak's Panther films are closer to Velvia in their colour rendition, and also use E-6 chemistry. Velvia is my first choice for insect close-ups, largely because pictures of colourful insects shot on this film really sock you in the eye. Despite this, some photographers still prefer the more muted hues of Kodachrome. I have heard it said that Kodachrome is 'truer to life', but in fact no film records every colour faithfully. They all have some sort of bias.

Although Kodak and Fuji dominate the market, Agfa and Konica also offer high-quality products. I suggest that you experiment with various films, and when you find one you like, stick with it. It's always an advantage to be familiar with your film.

This female Wolf spider was guarding her eggs in the midst of a dense tangle of grass stems, and I had to position the tripod and obtain a clear shot without disturbing her. A 180mm lens gave me plenty of working distance (about 40cm) and produced an uncluttered background.
180mm macro lens, 27.5mm extension tube, 1sec. at f/16.

EXPOSURE

Exposure theory must be one of the least appealing aspects of photography. After all, most of us take up photography because we want to take pictures, not because we are enthralled by the idea of finding out what an f-stop is. Learning the principles of exposure seems like a chore, and many people avoid it by relying on a programmed camera.

As I've already said, I don't think that any amount of clever program modes are a substitute for an understanding of exposure. If you wish to gain real control over how your pictures look, this is one area you must master. Fortunately, the principles involved are quite simple.

HOW EXPOSURE IS CONTROLLED

Achieving the proper exposure in a photograph means ensuring that the picture is neither too light (overexposed) nor too dark (underexposed). In order to achieve this, the correct amount of light has to reach the film, and it is controlled by two means. The first is the iris diaphragm of the lens, which works on the same optical principle as the iris in your eye. Its variable size regulates the volume of light that enters the camera: the larger the aperture, the more light the lens will admit. The second is the camera's shutter, whose variable speed determines the length of time for which the film is exposed to that light. 'Exposure' is a combination of light intensity and duration.

In order to control the exposure with enough accuracy, photographers measure differences in light intensity in units referred to as 'stops'. The aperture and shutter speed controls are both designed to regulate the light in stops, or fractions thereof. Each whole stop represents a doubling (or halving) of the light intensity reaching the film. The lens aperture is traditionally set via an aperture ring located on the lens barrel, although some camera manufacturers have dispensed with this in favour of a control located on the camera body. In either case, the adjustment of the aperture progresses in stops which are denoted by 'f-numbers'. A typical 100mm macro lens might offer the following range:

F/ 2.8	4	5.6	8	11	16	22	32

f/2.8 denotes the largest aperture, and f/32 the smallest.

Marbled White on toadflax. Remember that your camera's light meter is calibrated to provide an accurate light reading when it is directed at a middle-toned area. Here the frame is dominated by light tones, so I based my exposure on a separate meter reading taken from a grey card. 105mm macro lens, 1sec. at f/11.

There is a reason for the apparently puzzling progression of f-numbers. This is that each f-number represents the ratio between the focal length of the lens and the diameter of the aperture, so with the 100mm lens, f/4 indicates a 25mm aperture – not that you really need to remember this! The key points to appreciate are these:

- Small f-numbers denote large apertures, and therefore more light entering the camera. Conversely, large f-numbers denote small apertures and less light entering the camera.

- The f-number scale progresses in increments of one stop, i.e., each successive f-number represents a further halving of the light intensity.

Thus the lens aperture enables you to control exactly how much light enters the camera. In order to control the length of time for which the film is exposed to this light, the camera's shutter can be set at any one of a dozen or more pre-set speeds. A well-specified camera would offer at least the following range:

1/2000	1/1000	1/500	1/250	1/125	1/60
1/30	1/15	1/8	1/4	1/2	1	2	4	sec.

Green Grasshopper.
My standard procedure for setting the exposure manually is to select the aperture, then set the shutter speed in accordance with a light reading taken from a middle-toned reference point. In this case, I used the out-of-focus grass in the background as my reference.
105mm macro lens, 27.5mm extension tube. 1/4sec. at f/11.

Above left–
This shot of a brown hawker was taken with the dragonfly framed up as shown, and with the camera set to its aperture-priority mode. Much of the frame was a stop lighter than a middle tone, and the camera has wrongly interpreted this as an extra stop of light. The picture is underexposed by one stop as a result. *180mm macro lens, 1/2sec. at f/11.*

Above right–
Brown Hawker. Here I've repeated the shot using the same aperture, but this time I obtained an accurate light reading by metering a grey card. The shutter speed was then set manually, resulting in an accurate exposure. *180mm macro lens, 1sec. at f/11.*

Although we are now dealing with time, using fractions of a second, the scale of shutter speeds also progresses in one-stop increments. A one stop change in shutter speed affects the exposure to the same extent as a one stop change in aperture.

One result of this is that any adjustment that is made to one control can be offset by making an equivalent adjustment to the other. This means that in a given situation, it is possible to use any one of several different combinations of aperture and shutter speed. For example, if your camera indicates an exposure of 1/60sec. at f/5.6, you are not restricted to shooting at f/5.6. You can 'stop down' to f/8. This means you now have one stop less light entering the camera – but you can compensate by exposing the film for longer. If you set the shutter speed one stop slower to 1/30sec., the film will still be correctly exposed. Alternatively, you can go the other way and 'open up' the aperture by one stop to f/4. Now you have one stop more light entering the camera, so you must expose the film for less time. Setting the shutter speed one stop faster to 1/125sec. will give you the correct exposure.

Of course, this principle can be taken further. You can deviate from the original aperture by as many stops as the lens's aperture range will allow, as long as you also change the shutter speed by an equal number of stops to compensate. The same amount of light would reach the film if you set any one of the eight following exposures:

① 1/250sec. at f/2.8   ⑤ 1/15sec. at f/11
② 1/125sec. at f/4   ⑥ 1/8sec. at f/16
③ 1/60sec. at f/5.6   ⑦ 1/4sec. at f/22
④ 1/30sec. at f/8   ⑧ 1/2sec. at f/32

It's vital to have this ability to choose from a selection of possible exposures, because varying the aperture and/or shutter speed does not just determine how light or dark the photograph appears. It also determines how much depth of field there is in the picture, and it affects the way in which movement is portrayed. This is why I prefer to set the exposure manually, rather than set the camera on 'program' and let it take over what is a creative decision.

SETTING THE APERTURE

Each time I set an exposure, my first step is to select the lens aperture. Although you can work the other way around, i.e. setting the shutter speed first, I would suggest that with insect close-ups you make the aperture your main consideration. This is because the aperture determines how much depth of field there will be at any given magnification. This is a major concern in close-up photography because as the image magnification increases, the depth of field diminishes. If you increase the magnification enough to shoot worthwhile insect portraits, only a shallow area of the picture a few millimetres deep may appear sharp. With so little depth of field to work with it's particularly important that you control it effectively.

If you use the lens 'wide open', i.e. at its largest aperture setting, the depth of field will be at its most shallow, and the picture will look exactly as it appears in the viewfinder. If you 'stop down' to a smaller aperture, the depth of field increases, although you will only be able to see this increase in the viewfinder if your camera has a depth-of-field preview facility. This is because on modern lenses the aperture only closes down to the chosen setting just before the shutter fires. The idea of having it remain wide open until this point is to provide the brightest possible viewfinder image by which to focus. If you want to see how much depth of field you are going to get before you take the picture, you need a depth-of-field preview facility.

Mating Orange Tips.
In this shot, the central portion of the frame is dominated by the butterflies' wings, which are about one stop lighter than a middle tone. Had I simply framed the shot up and set the exposure recommended by the camera, the picture would have been underexposed by one stop, so I based the exposure on a light reading taken from the middle-toned background. 105mm macro lens, 1/2sec. at f/11.

I use the depth-of-field preview button every time I set the exposure for a natural-light close-up. Having framed the subject, I depress the button and work through the aperture settings until the picture looks right. Sometimes I may want just enough depth of field to ensure that the subject is sharp, while the background remains a muted blur. In order to emphasise the subject in this way I often find myself shooting at f/5.6 or f/8. If the background is particularly attractive, or relevant to the natural history of the subject, I may prefer to go for as much depth of field as possible, in which case f/22 might be more appropriate. The depth-of-field preview facility takes the guesswork out of selecting the aperture for any desired effect.

OBTAINING AN ACCURATE LIGHT READING

Having set the aperture, the next step is to match it with whatever shutter speed is appropriate to the amount of available light. In order to determine which shutter speed should be set you need to measure the available light with a light meter.

Meters can be divided into two basic types. Incident-light meters are hand-held and measure daylight directly. Reflected-light meters measure the light that is reflected by any surface at which they are aimed; whilst many hand-held meters offer this facility, the reflected-light meter which most photographers use is the one that is built into their camera.

In order to use your camera's meter to best effect, you should be aware that it is not infallible. In certain circumstances it will give an inaccurate light reading. The reason is that it does not measure the light directly; it measures reflected light, so it will be influenced by the tone of whatever surface you are metering. This is easy to demonstrate if you aim your camera at a succession of light and dark objects under the same illumination. The readings that you get vary considerably, but if the light isn't changing, then neither should the exposure; obviously the meter makes mistakes.

Fortunately, this is a simple problem to overcome. All you have to do is take your meter reading from an area which is middle-toned. As far as photography is concerned, the term 'middle-toned' has a precise connotation; it means anything of the same tone as an 18% grey, the tone used by camera manufacturers to calibrate light meters.

Conveniently enough, middle-toned surfaces are common

Above left–
Crab Spider on knapweed. Your choice of aperture will determine how much depth of field you have at any given magnification. At f/4, the depth of field is very shallow, so most of the knapweed flower is out of focus. *105mm macro lens, 1/15sec. f/4.*

Above right–
Crab Spider on knapweed. At f/22, there is ample depth of field for the knapweed flower, but I had to use an exposure time of 2s. Such long exposures are only practicable if the subject is completely still. *105mm macro lens, 2secs. at f/22.*

in nature. Most tree bark, fresh green grass and other vegetation of a similar hue can act as references from which you may obtain accurate light readings. Alternatively, you can carry a middle-toned reference area in your camera bag, namely a purpose-made 18% grey card. You can obtain one of these from any good photographic retailer. Do make sure that you obtain one which has a true matt finish, because any reflective sheen will catch the light and affect the meter reading.

If the subject and its surroundings are middle-toned, setting the right exposure is simplicity itself, because (depending on your camera's specification) you can rely on one of the most basic automatic exposure modes, 'aperture priority'. This allows you to select the aperture so that you control the depth of field, but the camera automatically sets the appropriate shutter speed.

It's possible to use aperture priority with subjects of almost any tone provided the camera has some provision for exposure compensation. Usually this takes the form of a dial graduated in fractions of a stop. An exposure compensation dial is really a means of telling the camera the true tone of whatever it is metering. For instance, if you are metering something which is one stop darker than a middle tone, you dial in -1. If you are metering something which is one stop lighter than a middle tone, you dial in +1, and so on.

Of course, to succeed consistently with this method, you need to be able to judge the tone of the subject with considerable accuracy. The margin for error with slide films is only a third of a stop. Unless you are prepared to bracket all your exposures – which is just a waste of film – I'd suggest that you adopt a method which doesn't rely on guesswork.

MANUAL EXPOSURE

Once you have selected the aperture and obtained a reliable light reading, you are only a short step from having complete manual exposure control. All you need do is set the shutter speed in accordance with the light reading, and shoot. To summarise, here is the procedure which I follow for about 90% of my natural light close-ups of insects:

1. Set up the shot to the point where the subject is framed and the lens is focused;

2. Select the camera's manual exposure mode, and either centre-weighted or spot metering*, preferably the latter as it will allow a reading to be taken from a very small area if necessary;

3. Select the lens aperture, checking the depth of field preview as previously described;

4. Without changing the focus, pan on to a grey card, or any other middle-toned area ensuring that this is under the same illumination as the subject;

5. Set the shutter speed recommended by the camera as it meters the middle tone;

6. Frame the subject once again and start shooting.

   *Canon EOS users should not select spot metering when using extension tubes.

With practice, this technique becomes second nature. It's infallible as long as you meter from a true middle tone which is under the same illumination as the subject.

It's important that once you have focused on the subject (step 1), no further adjustment should be made to the

Burnet Moth on scabious flower. With backlit subjects, metering a middle-toned reference point doesn't always work. Quite often you will need to underexpose the subject, perhaps to prevent the more brightly lit background from burning out, or to deliberately produce a silhouette or emphasise the rimlighting effect which sometimes occurs with backlighting.

The correct exposure for this shot was found as follows: First I selected the aperture to suit depth-of-field requirements in the normal way. I then took a spot meter reading from part of the background, having decided that this area ought to appear one stop lighter than a middle tone in the photograph. I set a shutter speed one stop slower than the one recommended by the camera. (Remember that the camera always recommends an exposure that will make whatever it is metering appear middletoned, whereas I wanted this area be be one stop lighter than that.) Finally, I recomposed and began shooting. 105mm macro lens, 1/60sec. at f/8.

focus throughout the whole process, other than the odd minor tweak as you are shooting. Remember that with most lenses, whenever you change the focus to any great extent you actually change the amount of extension being used and hence the amount of light which reaches the film at any given aperture.

Do bear in mind that you aren't restricted to making adjustments to the aperture in full stops. In order to allow finer control of the exposure (which is particularly important with slide film), the aperture ring can be set anywhere you choose, including part way between marked f-numbers. Some cameras, such as the Nikon F5 and F90X, also allow the shutter speed to be manually controlled in fractions of a stop. This enables you to fine-tune the exposure without adjusting the aperture setting.

EXPOSING FOR BACKLIT SUBJECTS

If the subject is backlit, i.e., lit from directly behind, you may need to adopt a slightly different approach when setting the exposure. The problem is that the subject is in shadow, so it may be the least well-lit part of the picture.

There are two kinds of backlighting: the deliberate kind, and the kind that you have to put up with simply because it isn't possible to shoot from a better viewpoint! In the latter case, the obvious thing to do is to add some extra light to the subject so that the picture will be more evenly lit. I normally do this with a reflector, in which case setting the exposure is simple. Just follow the method described above, ensuring you take the light reading from a middle tone which, like the subject, is backlit but also illuminated by the reflector. Alternatively, use fill-in flash, although this may look a little out of place. Flash light is cooler and whiter than sunlight, and harsher than overcast light.

What if you are intentionally shooting so that the subject is backlit? This can be an excellent way of producing insect close-ups that are quite different from the run of the mill. For some reason, most photographers don't consider shooting silhouettes or featuring rim-lighting effects when photographing insects. My usual technique here is to base the exposure on a meter reading taken from part of the background. The area being metered need not be middle-toned, provided you can make an accurate estimate of the tone that it should be in the final image. For example, let's say the background is filled with of out-of-focus highlights from sunlit dewy grass. Such a bright background should be about two stops lighter than a middle tone. Therefore you should match the aperture with a shutter speed that the camera indicates will overexpose by two stops. What if the background is darker? You might wish to emphasise a rim-lighting effect by shooting a backlit insect against a background of shadow. If you want the background to be about one stop darker than a middle tone, you should set a shutter speed that the camera indicates will underexpose by one stop.

Basically this method relies on educated guesswork, so you'd be well advised to bracket up to one stop either side of your estimated exposure to guarantee success. Given

Meadow Brown on Reed.
The meadow brown is rather
a drab butterfly, and
I photographed this one
during the summer of 1995
when the meadows of
southern England had been
parched by drought. Without
any real colour contrast to
help separate the butterfly
from its background, the only
way to make the shot work
was to keep the background
completely out of focus.
Using the camera's depth of
field preview facility,
I selected f/8 as the aperture
which would ensure a sharp
subject and a clean, blank
background. 180mm macro
lens, 1/4sec. at f/8.

that you are likely to use this method for only a minority of your pictures, this won't involve wasting much film.

SHUTTER SPEED AND MOVEMENT

Although I've suggested that you should normally give priority to the lens aperture, it is also important to consider the effect of varying the shutter speed. The main point here is the way in which movement is portrayed at different shutter speeds. If the subject moves during the exposure, it will be blurred in the photograph. The longer the exposure and the more the movement, the more pronounced this effect will be.

If you regularly shoot insect close-ups using natural light, you soon get used to using slow shutter speeds. This is the result of a combination of factors. Firstly, this technique generally works best early and late in the day, because you need inactive subjects. As a result, you start out with quite low light levels. Usually it's necessary to use small lens apertures to get enough depth of field, and the amount of light reaching the film may be further reduced by accessories such as extension tubes or a teleconverter. If you also use a slow film (which many photographers prefer, in order to do justice to the fine detail of the subject),

53

you'll rarely find yourself using a shutter speed faster than about 1/15sec. This makes it almost impossible to get sharp results with a moving subject, and wind movement is a major problem.

However, marginal situations sometimes arise whereby it can pay to compromise a little on your 'ideal' aperture. For example, having shielded and steadied a frail subject as much as possible, you may find that you have all but eliminated the effects of a light breeze. It may be that by opening up a stop you can actually get a viable exposure. Using a shutter speed of say, 1/8sec. instead of 1/4sec. may make just enough difference to get you a sharp result. The accompanying loss of a little depth of field is something you just have to live with.

In really poor light, such a compromise would not be worthwhile. The original shutter speed may be so low that gaining one stop won't help much; where wind movement is concerned, two-second exposures aren't much better than four-second exposures. In these circumstances I tend to accept defeat gracefully, and retire to the nearest cafe for a hearty breakfast!

Marbled White basking. One of the best times to photograph butterflies is when they are basking in the first rays of the morning sun. Many species will remain motionless with open wings for several minutes before making their first flight. 180mm macro lens, 1/30sec. at f/8.

This Ringlet was originally roosting on a dead grass stem that had little appeal from a photographic point of view, so I coaxed the sleepy butterfly on to a twig, and transferred it on to this clover flower. If you manipulate a shot in this way you must make sure that you don't set up a situation which would not occur naturally. Immediately after photographing the ringlet I returned it to its original perch. 180mm macro lens, 1/15sec. at f/11.

MAGNIFICATION

It is natural to assume that in close-up photography, the closer you can get to the subject, the better. In fact, getting particularly close to your subject is not an end in itself. The closer you are, the more critical the positioning of the camera will be, and the more difficulty you will have in trying to photograph subjects which are easily disturbed.

The close-up photographer's real aim is to obtain enough image magnification; in other words, to ensure that the subject is large enough in the frame, which is not necessarily the same thing as getting in close. More often than not, with insects, the aim is to obtain enough magnification whilst staying as far away as possible!

Magnification is measured by relating the size of the subject's image on film to its actual size in life. A convenient example would be a frame-filling portrait of a small butterfly which is basking with open wings. Let's say it has a wingspan of 30mm. In order to virtually fill the frame on a 35mm negative or transparency, its image will need to be about 30mm across - the same size as the living insect. In other words, it's image would be life-size, and this is the term that photographers use. If the butterfly were shot so as to appear only half as big in the frame, making its image half the size of the living insect, the magnification would be 'half life-size'. Different magnifications are variously expressed as one-third life-size, one-quarter life-size and so on. Alternatively, a particular magnification may be expressed as a reproduction ratio, which is the ratio between the size of the image and the size of the subject. In technical literature, life-size is denoted by '1:1', half life-size by '1:2', one-third life size by '1:3' and so on.

Whenever close-up photographers refer to magnification, they use one or other of these terms, and the distance from which the picture was taken remains more or less irrelevant. For instance, if you were to shoot the life-size butterfly portrait with a 100mm macro lens, you would need to be about 16cm away, but by changing lenses and using various accessories, you could easily shoot from the same distance and end up with anything from one quarter to twice life-size (1:4–2:1) The butterfly could be far too small, or bursting out of the frame! This is why it is the magnification that matters, not how close you are.

Brown Hawker. My original intention was to shoot the dragonfly in its entirety. This would have been well within the capabilities of my 180mm macro lens which reaches half life-size on its own. However, close inspection revealed that one of the dragonfly's wings was damaged. In order to exclude the tattered wing, I began playing around with much tighter compositions which required more magnification. I swapped the 180mm for a 105mm macro and 52.5mm extension tube to reach just over life-size, sufficient to shoot this head-and-thorax portrait. Ironically, the final result was more interesting than the picture I'd first had in mind!
105mm macro lens, 52.5mm extension tube, 4secs. at f/16.

HOW MUCH MAGNIFICATION DO YOU NEED?

When you find a potential subject in the field, you don't have to make precise calculations as to its size and the exact magnification which will be required. As with any form of photography, you decide how large the subject ought to appear by assessing what you see in the viewfinder and settling on whatever looks right. However, with experience, you will probably acquire a feel for magnification, and you will immediately know roughly what will be required for each shot.

The most useful range of magnification starts at about one-quarter life-size, or 1:4, at which point you could start to get worthwhile results with large butterflies or dragonflies. In order to shoot frame-fillers of smaller creatures, your outfit should ideally be capable of reaching life-size. At 1:1 a tremendous range of subjects comes within reach, and you will rarely need to exceed this magnification unless you wish to specialise in very tiny subjects or head-and-shoulders type insect portraits. For this type of work you may need to reach at least twice life-size, or 2:1, which is about as far as you can go in the field. All the usual difficulties that are inherent in close-up work are aggravated as magnification increases, and at twice

Broad-Bodied Chaser on bramble. If possible, I try to avoid bisecting the frame with a straight line, especially a horizontal or a vertical. Here I've rotated the camera slightly to turn what was a straight-and-level bramble stem into a diagonal. With no horizon to refer to, no-one would ever know!
300mm IF-ED lens with 52.5mm and 27.5mm extension tubes, 1/30sec. at f/5.6.

Green Leafhopper on bramble leaf. At barely 8mm long, this tiny subject required plenty of magnification simply to ensure that it would be large enough in the frame. By combining my macro lens with an extension tube and supplementary, I was able to reach 1 1/2 x life-size.
105mm macro lens with 52.5mm extension tube and Nikon 4T, 1/250sec. at f/16.

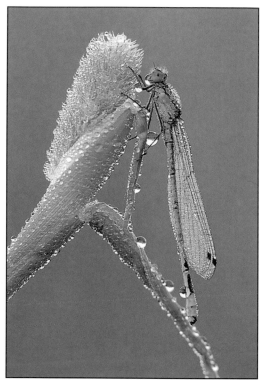

life-size or beyond it is very difficult to work in anything less than ideal conditions. This is why most high-magnification photography is carried out in the studio.

OBTAINING ENOUGH MAGNIFICATION

About 80% of my insect photographs are shot at between 1:3 and 1:1, and this range of magnification falls within the capabilities of quite a basic outfit. If you own a macro lens, the chances are that it will reach 1:1 on its own, unless it is an older design, in which case a more modest 1:2 is likely to be its maximum. The simplest way to improve on this is to add an extension tube. In fact, with most fixed focal length lenses, adding extension is the simplest way of reaching magnifications of up to 1:1. Exactly how much you will need in order to reach 1:1 depends on the focal length of the lens. Any lens will produce a magnification of 1:1 when the total amount of extension used is equal to the lens's focal length. In other words, if you mount a 100mm lens on 100mm of extension, it will produce a life-size image. Bear in mind that most lenses have a certain amount of extension built in to their focusing mounts. Typically a conventional 100mm lens might have about

Above left–
This damselfly was photographed with a 50mm lens. Because of the comparatively wide angle of view at this focal length, it was impossible to prevent the distracting strip of sky from intruding into the top of the frame. The 50mm also forced me to work too close to the subject - about 12cm away. *50mm lens with 14mm extension tube, 1sec. at f/11.*

Above right–
The whole exercise was much easier with a 180mm lens. Its narrow field of view made it easy to exclude the sky, producing a cleaner background, and the extra focal length provided much more working distance; the damselfly posed happily while I shot from about 40cm away. *180mm macro lens, 1sec. at f/11.*

20mm built in, so if you set it at its closest focus, another 80mm would be required to reach life-size.

Macro lenses invariably have a lot more built-in extension. This may be further enhanced by an internal focusing system, whereby certain optical elements move individually during focusing. A 100mm macro which can reach 1:2 on its own will have the equivalent of 50mm built in, so it will only require an extra 50mm to reach life-size.

The more extension you add to an outfit, the more difficult it becomes to use. This means that if you wish to reach 1:1 with a conventional lens of much more than 100mm, just adding extension is not the best solution. A 200mm lens would require 200mm of extension to reach 1:1, at least 180mm of which would have to be added in the form of tubes or a bellows unit. In either case you would have a very cumbersome outfit, and the numerous joints between the various accessories would make it prone to vibration. Using such a system in the field wouldn't be a very practical proposition.

Whenever the focal length of the lens and/or the need for more magnification demands an impractical amount of extension (by which I mean more than about 80mm) I would use a supplementary lens or a teleconverter.

Normally I would opt for a supplementary rather than a teleconverter, because as well as being more compact, it does not reduce the amount of light reaching the film. It can also produce a marked improvement in magnification. For instance, a typical 200mm lens and 50mm tube will reach a maximum of about two-fifths life-size, or 1:2.5. The working distance between lens and subject is about 83cm. If you add Nikon's 4T supplementary, the maximum magnification leaps to about 1:0.8, well over life-size. The working distance drops to only 23cm, but this is still respectable for such a magnification.

Working distance is the one factor which sometimes makes a teleconverter the best choice, because when you add a teleconverter, you get more magnification without having to move closer to the subject. If you add a X2 converter to the 200mm lens and 50mm tube, the maximum magnification is doubled to four-fifths life-size (1:1.25), while the working distance remains 83cm. This could be a great advantage with an inaccessible subject, or one which is likely to flee if you make a close approach. Nevertheless, this is an outfit that I would tend to use as a last resort, because the converter robs you of two stops of light, which

Honeybee and pollen. The bee was taking a breather between shifts. Its surroundings weren't particularly attractive, so I decided to shoot a tight portrait that would feature the pollen on the bee's body. *I added an extension tube and a supplementary to my macro lens, shooting at about 1¹/₂x life-size.* 105mm macro lens with 52.5mm extension tube and Nikon 4T supplementary, 1/250sec. at f/16 with flash.

Bumblebee in bindweed flower. This is another shot which depends on plenty of magnification for its impact. I mounted my 105mm macro lens on a 52.5mm extension tube and fitted a X1.6 teleconverter between this and the camera. The result is a maximum magnification of just over 1¹/₂x life size. I used flash to freeze the excessive camera shake which occurs when you hand-hold the camera at high magnifications. 105mm macro lens with 52.5mm extension tube and X1.6 teleconverter, 1/250sec. at f/16 with flash.

makes for very slow shutter speeds and a dim viewfinder image. By doubling the focal length, it also makes the outfit extremely sensitive to vibration. If you combine an extension tube with a teleconverter, you will find that fitting the tube between the converter and the lens will yield more magnification than fitting the converter between the tube and the camera.

There are other ways of reaching high magnifications, most of which are best suited to studio photography. Set-ups which are based on short lenses, reverse-mounted lenses and bellows units are usually too awkward or inconvenient for use in the field.

COMPOSITION

If your goal is to produce outstanding pictures, developing a fine sense of composition should be a priority. Technical perfection in terms of exposure and sharpness is certainly important, but on its own it will not guarantee anything more than a competent record shot.

The aesthetic appeal of a picture usually has much to do with its composition: where the subject is placed in the frame, how large it is in the frame, its orientation, and how it relates to other aspects of the picture. These qualities are just as important in close-ups of insects as they are in any other kind of photography.

As a starting point, beware of the temptation to make the subject as large as possible in the frame. If you are trying to produce a dramatic portrait showing the bizarre detail of an insect's face, it's fine to have the subject bursting out of the picture. Such a shot will rely on the high magnification for its impact. However, if you are after a more subtle aesthetic effect, it is restrictive to have the subject filling the frame; you are left with little option other than to simply cram it in as best you can. There is no room for the viewer's eye to explore the space around the subject, nor can you give any impression of its habitat.

Grey Dagger on brickwork. Although I usually try to exclude man-made elements from my pictures, the brickwork was too tempting a background to ignore - and as far as the moth is concerned, a brick wall is just another part of its natural environment. The brickwork divides the picture horizontally and vertically, while the only diagonal element is the subject. Fortunately, the moth had settled in a position which lent itself to a pleasing composition, with the line of the mortar following part of the 'rule of thirds' grid.
105mm macro lens with 52.5mm extension tube, 1/250sec. at f/11 with flash.

There is one other seemingly obvious point to consider when you are working out how to compose a picture. Always ask yourself whether the subject is better suited to a portrait (vertical) or landscape (horizontal) composition. Many photographers habitually shoot in landscape format, which is a pity. Some subjects cry out to be shot in portrait format (insects on vertical plant stems often fall into this category) and this type of framing does intrigue the eye, perhaps because we see it less often.

COMPOSITIONAL AIDS

Composing a picture is primarily a creative process not bound by hard-and-fast rules, such as those which govern exposure. Nevertheless it is still possible to make mistakes, and a badly composed picture looks 'wrong' as soon as you set eyes on it. Fortunately there are some useful rules of thumb that can help when you find yourself pondering

Marbled white on scabious. Another shot which required only a moderate amount of magnification because I wanted to include the butterfly's surroundings rather than go in close for a frame-filling portrait. The magnification here is about one quarter life-size.
200mm lens with 52.5mm extension tube, 1/30sec. at f/8.

over what you see in the viewfinder. The most widely used of these is the 'rule of thirds', which pinpoints key areas within the frame sometimes referred to as 'points of power'. When a subject is placed on one of these points the effect tends to be more dynamic and pleasing to the eye than if it is simply planted centrally in the picture. Using the rule of thirds is simply a matter of mentally superimposing a grid on to the frame, made up of two vertical and two horizontal lines. These lines divide the frame into thirds, both horizontally and vertically, and the four points at which they intersect are the 'points of power'. Compare the diagram on this page with the photograph opposite.

Crab spider on knapweed flower. Having decided to keep the spider fairly small in the frame so as to make a feature of the vivid purple petals, I used the rule of thirds, framing the spider so that it lies on one of the 'points of power', looking down into the frame. Its conspicuous colour ensures that it is not overshadowed by the gaudy flower.
105mm macro lens, 52.5mm extension tube, 2secs. at f/16.

Don't feel that you have to follow the rule of thirds rigidly. Look upon it as an aid rather than a rule, and employ it quite loosely. Some photographers and artists use an alternative rule known as the golden mean, which was devised by the ancient Greeks. It is also based on four points of power, but places them slightly closer to the centre of the frame. A close approximation to their position is two-fifths in from the picture's edges.

There is another point to bear in mind when you opt for an off-centre positioning of the subject. When we look at a picture of an animal of any kind we tend to be more interested in what is in front of it than in what is behind it. The area behind almost becomes 'dead space'. This should become apparent if you note where your eye travels as you look at such a picture. When it leaves the subject it naturally tends to jump ahead, as if to see where the subject is going or what it is looking at. With this in mind, it is usually more effective to place an off-centre subject so that it faces into the picture – even if it does happen to have compound eyes, and may actually be looking in many different directions at once!

Although a central positioning of the subject often results in a rather lifeless effect which does not hold the viewer's eye, it can suit certain subjects very nicely. An obvious

Flesh fly. A subject like this doesn't have much going for it from an aesthetic point of view; most people just find it repulsive. I decided the best approach would be to play on this, so I shot a frame filler at 1½ times life size. The more grotesque your subject, the better this type of shot will work.
105mm macro lens with 52.5mm extension tube and Nikon 4T supplementary, 1/250sec. at f/16 with flash.

***Spider in primula flower.
This spider is quite a drab
subject, but fortunately it
stopped in the middle of a
domestic primula, which has
added some welcome colour
to the picture.***
*105mm macro lens with
27.5mm extension tube,
1/250sec. at f/16 with flash.*

example would be a head-on portrait, or any subject which lends itself to a symmetrical composition. Shooting down on to an insect (or part of one) from directly above is one way of producing this type of shot.

Another tried and trusted photographic rule of thumb says that you should avoid bisecting the frame with a straight vertical or horizontal line. In landscape photography for instance, the classic example would be a straight horizon bisecting the picture. With insect close-ups, it's rarely possible to see a well defined horizon. Instead, you are more likely to get the same effect from the edge of a leaf or a plant stem cutting across the frame. If the offending vegetation is simply part of the background it's sometimes possible to exclude it by temporarily tying it back with twine. This is not practical in close proximity to a flighty subject, nor is it much use if your insect is actually sitting on the eyesore in question! In this case, see if you can shoot from a different angle.

A small change in the position or orientation of the camera can work wonders. A simple example would be a shot of an insect clinging to a vertical plant stem. If you rotate the camera slightly so as to divide the frame with a slightly diagonal stem instead of a vertical, the effect is more

Above–
Southern Hawker on withered nettle. Although this pristine hawker is a wonderful subject, it hasn't made a great picture because of the unsightly background. *105mm macro lens, 1/250sec. at f/11 with flash.*

Left–
Marbled White and seedheads. I was immediately attracted by the entwined seedheads which this butterfly had chosen for its overnight roost. As well as helping to convey the impression of high summer in an English meadow, they have attractive textures and fit nicely into the frame. *105mm macro lens with 27.5mm extension tube. 1/4sec. at f/11.*

Right–
Marbled White butterfly. Rather than go in close for a frame-filler of the butterfly, I made its perch an important element. I liked the way the dewy seed heads were glistening in the first glimmer of sunlight, and the fact that their size and shape made a balanced composition. *105mm macro lens, 1/15sec. at f/8.*

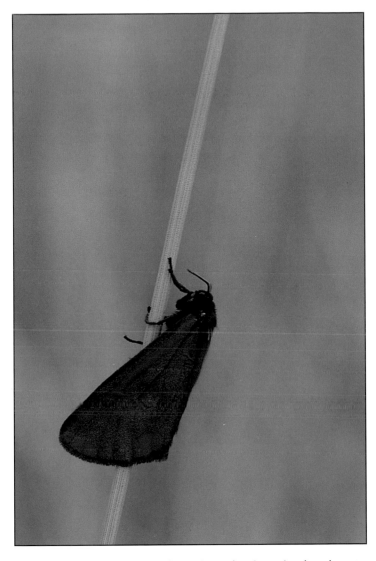

Cinnabar Moth. A simple composition which is loosely based on the rule of thirds.
105mm macro lens with 52.5mm extension tube, 1/2sec. at f/8.

Cinnabar caterpillar feeding on ragwort. Consider the effect of colour when you are composing a picture. Certain colours, particularly red, orange and yellow immediately command our attention and will make a subject stand out. The colouration of this cinnabar caterpillar is designed to make it conspicuous to predators and warn them that it is poisonous.
180mm macro lens, 52.5mm extension tube, 1/4sec. at f/8.

pleasing, and as long as there is no horizon in the shot to provide a reference, no one can tell that the stem wasn't growing at an angle anyway.

One other gremlin that will regularly try to creep into your pictures is the background hotspot, an out-of-focus highlight which contributes nothing to the picture other than to distract the eye from the subject. Such hotspots may result from portions of sky appearing along the top edge of the frame, pale flowers or litter in the background, or areas which are more brightly illuminated than the subject. If you are shooting a shaded subject in otherwise bright conditions with natural light, this last one is often a problem. Try not to be so intent on the subject that you don't notice these distractions, because they always appear worse in the photograph than they did in the viewfinder. Whenever you appraise what you see in the viewfinder, look at the picture you are taking, not just the subject.

This principle of thinking in terms of the entire picture also applies when you are looking for subjects. Assuming that you are aiming for something more than just a record shot, don't be content to photograph anything you can get close to. The majority of insects which you come across won't be particularly well placed from a photographic point of view, and time spent on photographing them might be better spent in looking for more exceptional pictures where nature has given you a head start. Nature is full of patterns and shapes that can enhance your pictures.

Having neatly presented the conventional wisdom on composition, I hope it will not confuse the issue if I say that all of these rules were made to be broken. I suspect that you will do well to follow them initially, but as you become more experienced, do experiment. Composing a picture is supposed to be a creative process, and you should always look for ways of introducing elements of originality into your pictures.

Right–
Miller Moth on tree bark. The textures and patterns in bark make an excellent background. *105mm macro lens with 52.5mm extension tube, 2secs. at f/16.*

Left–
Damselfly on reed. This picture was taken at first light in mid-May, during a visit to a small lake on a local farm. I found the damselfly clinging to a reed at the water's edge, where it was perfectly situated to shoot against the water. With the lake veiled in mist and the air perfectly still, the background is simply a grey void. The appeal of this shot lies in the simplicity of its composition. *105mm macro lens, 1/4sec. at f/8.*

FLASH PHOTOGRAPHY

Electronic flash supplies the photographer with a superabundance of light, making very short exposures possible even when using slow films and small lens apertures at high image magnifications. Such exposures enable you to tackle active subjects, and they eliminate all but the most frenzied cases of camera shake, so you can hand-hold the camera. It's therefore not surprising that flash is so widely used for photographing insects.

Flash has one or two disadvantages, mainly in terms of the quality of the lighting that it provides. Many photographers don't worry too much about this, but generally I much prefer the more subtle and natural effects which result from using daylight. As a result, only a small proportion of my insect close-ups are shot with flash, and I use it purely as a means of obtaining shots that would not be possible with natural light alone. I never use it simply for its convenience.

In order to understand the advantages and disadvantages associated with flash, it's necessary to consider what actually happens when you make a flash exposure.

When you trigger the camera, the shutter opens before the flash fires. The flash fires and dies away, usually in the space of 1/1000sec. or less, and the shutter then closes. A key point is that if the shot is lit solely by the flash, the shutter speed is largely irrelevant; it is the duration of the flash which determines the effective exposure duration. I invariably use flash in conjunction with a slow film, a small lens aperture, and with the camera set to the fastest shutter speed that will synchronise with the flash. The result is that the image is indeed made entirely by the flash; no daylight registers on the film at all. This is not surprising if you consider the exposure which you would have to set for a daylight shot, and compare it with the flash exposure. On a fairly bright day, using an ISO50 film and an aperture of say, f/16, a meter reading for a daylight exposure would indicate a shutter speed of about 1/8sec. (I'm assuming that up to two stops of light are lost to extension as you focus down to 1:1.) Compare that shutter speed with the one you use with the flash at the same aperture. The camera's fastest synch speed is probably

Hoverflies in a poppy.
This poppy was one of many growing in an exposed situation along the edge of a field of wheat. The picture was taken during a breezy July morning, when wind movement made it impossible to use slow daylight exposures. The flash enabled me to freeze the movement of the poppy and still get plenty of depth of field. 105mm macro lens with 52.5mm extension tube, 1/250sec. at f/16 with flash.

1/125 or 1/250sec. This is four or five stops faster, so the daylight image is effectively being underexposed by four or five stops.

With no daylight registering on film, it follows that any area of the shot that is not illuminated by the flash will be swallowed up in deep shadow. One result of this can be a completely black background, an effect which arises whenever there is nothing immediately behind the subject for the flash to illuminate. It must be said that not everyone dislikes black backgrounds. Some people like them, possibly because they make the subject stand out so well. To me, a picture with a black background looks unnatural (except with nocturnal creatures), and it certainly isn't representative of the shot as it originally appeared in the viewfinder.

It's possible to estimate with accuracy how well illuminated your background will be. The illumination of an object depends on its distance from the light source according to a rule which relates directly to the scale of f-numbers.

As a convenient example, let's say that the distance between flash and subject is 16cm, as it would be when shooting at about life-size with a 100mm lens. An object of similar tone would appear one stop darker than the subject

Red Admiral. This butterfly was basking at head height in a bramble bush, and the nearest background vegetation was about two metres beyond it. As a result, only the subject has been illuminated by the flash, and the background is lost in a black void. Bear in mind that as the separation of background and light source increases, the illumination falls off rapidly. A burst of flash which is adequate to expose a butterfly correctly at a range of 30cm or so will not register on film at all by the time the light has travelled 2m.

105mm macro lens with 27.5mm extension tube, 1/250sec. at f/11 with flash.

Fairy Moth. The amazing 'gold leaf' iridescence of the fairy moth shows up well when illuminated by flash. Because I also wanted to show the incredibly long antennae, I had to keep the moth fairly small in the frame.
105mm macro lens with 27.5mm extension tube, 1/250sec. at f/16 with flash.

at 22cm, and two stops darker at 32cm (f/22 and f/32 being respectively one and two stops darker than f/16). As a rule of thumb, you can say that any middle-toned background object such as green foliage will record as black whenever the distance between subject and background exceeds the distance between flash and subject.

Of course, it is possible to blend flash with daylight by setting a slower shutter speed and/or larger aperture. In many areas of photography this is a widely-used technique, and it eliminates the problem of black backgrounds. It is ideal when you just need a little extra light to fill in some shadows but from the insect photographer's point of view the main advantage of flash is lost. You are back to slow daylight exposures, and with a moving subject the final result is usually an unsightly double image - a sharp but translucent flash image, merging with a darker and decidedly blurred daylight image.

Using multiple flashes is another way around the problem. If you use two or three units, one can be positioned so as to illuminate the background and triggered via a remote lead or slave unit, but this means you no longer have a fast-handling outfit with which to chase moving insects. The use of multiple flash arrangements is generally restricted to

Small White butterfly on herb Robert. An example of a fleeting moment which could not have been captured with a daylight exposure. The butterfly was moving rapidly from one flower to the next, and would waltz from side to side flexing its wings whilst feeding. The brief burst of flash (less than 1/1000sec.) has frozen these movements, and its proboscis can be seen draining nectar from the flower. +1 stop of exposure compensation was used to allow for the influence of its white wings on the TTL metering. 105mm macro lens, 1/250sec. at f/16 with flash.

situations where you can set up beforehand and wait for insects to come to you.

It is possible to buy multiple flash brackets which supposedly enable you to hand-hold the camera with three flashes fitted. Each flash is mounted on the end of a long flexible arm, the idea being that you position the outfit so that the subject is correctly framed and frontally lit by two of the flashes, whilst the third flash is behind it lighting the background. Of course, you have to get everything into place without disturbing your insect or snagging the surrounding vegetation, which must be quite a feat. I would probably end up throwing the whole outfit into the bushes out of sheer frustration!

Shield Bug in Lavatera flower. This is an ideal flash subject, because the immediate background (the flower) fills the entire frame. No danger of a black background here.
105mm macro lens with 52.5mm extension tube, 1/250sec. at f/16 with flash.

Longhorn beetle. If the frame is dominated by particularly light or dark tones, some exposure compensation will be necessary to obtain an accurate TTL flash exposure. As with daylight exposures, the camera's meter assumes that everything is supposed to appear middle-toned. In this case, it would have cut off the flash as soon as it had supplied enough light to make the daisy middle-toned, thereby under-exposing the picture. In order to avert this error, I dialled in +1 1/3 stops compensation.
105mm macro lens with 52.5mm extension tube, 1/250sec. at f/16 with flash.

For me, the whole point of using flash is to get a fast-handling outfit which can be used almost on a point-and-shoot basis. It should enable you to grab shots from quite fleeting opportunities, such as the few seconds when a bee or butterfly is taking nectar from a flower. An outfit based on a single bracket-mounted flash excels in this respect.

In order to avoid black backgrounds I just try to avoid photographing badly-placed subjects. Generally I look for shots where the flash will pick up flowers or vegetation in the background so as to produce a reasonably natural effect. Sometimes it's possible to add a background of your own by clamping a sprig of vegetation in a 'third arm' and positioning it close enough behind the subject. Of course, this only works with tolerant subjects.

A SIMPLE FLASH OUTFIT

My own flash outfit is a copy of John Shaw's 'butterfly bracket' set-up. It consists of a single conventional flash unit mounted on a home-made bracket. Being a Nikon user, I employ the Nikon SB-23, which is small, has a rapid recycling time, and, most usefully of all, offers TTL metering, invaluable for quick shooting. The flash is linked to the camera's hotshoe via its TTL cord, and sits just above the front of the lens, set at a shallow downward angle so as to directly illuminate subjects in the region of 15-30cm in front of the lens.

A simple flash-bracket outfit. The flash is a conventional TTL unit, chosen mainly for its small size. It is mounted on a simple home-made bracket, made by bending and drilling a short length of aluminium strip. This is secured to the tripod bush of the Nikon's 52.5mm extension tube, and supports the flash over the front of the lens, angled down at the subject.

FLASH BRACKETS

I use two varieties of home-made flash bracket. Both are made from lengths of 30mm wide x 3mm thick aluminium

Honeybee on dandelion. Bees can be surprisingly difficult to photograph because they are constantly on the move. It would have been impossible to photograph this one without flash. I needed the portability of a hand-held outfit to get into position before it flew on to the next flower, plus the action-stopping effect of the flash to freeze its movements.
105mm macro lens with 52.5mm extension tube, 1/250sec. at f/16 with flash.

strip, which is flexible enough to be bent into shape, but rigid enough to support a small flash. The simpler of the two is designed for use with lenses that have rotating tripod bushes, or with any lens used with Nikon's PNII extension tube. (This tube has its own tripod bush). The bracket is formed from a single length of strip bent in two places, and drilled with a single 1/4in. clearance hole at each end. These holes provide for the bracket to be secured to the tripod bush, and for the hotshoe of the TTL cable to be secured to the bracket.

Other than its simplicity, the beauty of this bracket is that being mounted on the tripod bush of the lens, it can easily be rotated in order to remain above the lens when you turn the camera on its side for a portrait-format shot. If this were not possible, all of my portrait-format shots would end up sidelit.

Do bear in mind that the extra weight of the flash places additional stress on the lens mount. It's advisable to handle such an outfit with one hand supporting the lens, in order to preclude any possibility of damaging the mount. This advice is particularly relevant if you are using one of the heavier 180 or 200mm macro lenses.

My other bracket is a two-piece design, and it is intended for use with lenses which have no tripod bush. It is also constructed from aluminium strip, and is secured into the tripod bush underneath the camera. It incorporates a small ball-and-socket tripod head that allows the position of the flash to be changed for portrait-format shooting, or to take into account variations in the amount of extension being used.

USING TTL-CONTROLLED FLASH

The TTL facility does away with any need for tricky exposure calculations, and enables you to shoot at any one of several lens apertures.

When the flash is set to its TTL mode, its duration is variable and is controlled by the camera's metering system. The camera actually meters the subject as the flash fires, and when enough light has been supplied to expose it correctly, the flash is automatically quenched.

This has to be an extremely rapid process, given that the duration of the flash may be well under 1/1000sec. It is pushed to its limits when the flash is placed within 30cm of the subject, because the level of light required for a correct exposure is reached much more quickly than normal. The result can be that with large lens apertures (which admit a

Hoverfly in flight. Conventional flash equipment has the ability to freeze a certain amount of movement, but don't expect it to work miracles; it won't produce incredible pictures of insects in flight. In this shot it has eliminated any camera shake, and the movement of the hoverfly's body, but there was no chance of freezing its wingbeats! 105mm macro lens with 27.5mm extension tube, 1/250sec. at f/16 with flash.

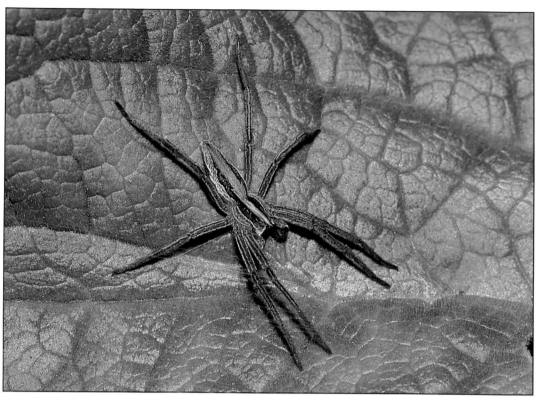

Wolf Spider.
Flash photographs don't have to be shadow-free. Shadows define texture; in this shot, the use of a single flash (rather than a ringflash) has produced just enough shadow to emphasise the texture of the leaf.
105mm macro lens with 52.5mm extension tube, 1/250sec. at f/16 with flash.

lot of light) the film gets overexposed before the camera has a chance to cut the flash.

Fortunately, this problem doesn't arise if you reduce the illumination at the film by setting a smaller aperture. With most small flashes correct TTL exposures are possible between f/8 and f/16, and depending on how much light you may be losing to accessories such as extension tubes or a teleconverter, you may get away with f/22 as well. Conveniently, this is the most useful range of apertures for shooting insect close-ups.

When using TTL flash, you should bear in mind that, as with daylight exposures, the camera's meter may be misled by subjects which are significantly lighter or darker than a middle tone. The camera will try to make the flash supply enough light to make whatever is being metered appear middle-toned on film, regardless of its true tone. It will thus underexpose lighter subjects and overexpose darker ones. The solution here is to use the exposure compensation dial, just as you would when shooting daylight exposures in aperture-priority mode. Again, you have to think in stops, dialling in + values for lighter subjects, and − values for darker ones.

Small Heath on bramble
flower. Sometimes black
backgrounds are
unavoidable. This small heath
was photographed during
the heat of the day and was
constantly on the move.
I couldn't blend the flash
with daylight, nor could
I move in some vegetation
behind it to make a 'fake'
background. I placed the
butterfly towards the top of
the frame so that much of
the shot would be filled by
its foodplant.
105mm macro lens with
52.5mm extension tube,
1/250sec. at f/16 with flash.

Opposite top–
Mating shield bugs.
One drawback with flash is
that as you look through the
viewfinder, you don't see the
shot as it will appear when
flashlit. Here the curve of the
rhubarb leaf has caught the
flash and reflected it back
into the lens, producing
a strong highlight which
distracts the viewer's eye
from the subjects.
105mm macro lens with
52.5mm extension tube,
1/250sec. at f/16 with flash.

Opposite below–
Pine Weevil. I found this
bizarre insect crawling
purposefully along the
windowsill by my back door.
He was in no mood to be
delayed, and I had to
photograph him at full
gallop. Once again the flash
was indispensable.
105mm macro lens with
52.5mm extension tube,
1/250sec. at f/11.

When you are estimating how much compensation to use, remember that you should compensate for the tone of whatever the camera is metering. This may not necessarily be the subject. For instance, you may be photographing a white butterfly, but if it is quite small in the frame and placed well off centre, it will not be influencing the meter to any great extent. Therefore, much less compensation would be required than if it were filling the frame.

If your camera has an advanced evaluative or matrix metering system, you should find that it will produce an acceptably high proportion of accurate TTL exposures without the need for any compensation. This can be a boon if you find it difficult to judge the tone value of different subjects, and as a result have a problem in compensating accurately.

MODIFYING YOUR FOCUSING TECHNIQUE

Using the flash bracket outfit in the field requires a focusing technique slightly different from the one that you would normally use. When shooting hand-held close-ups, you will find that as you approach the subject, the viewfinder image is usually completely out of focus, and this makes it very difficult to tell when you are at the right distance to shoot. Relying on guesswork, i.e. stopping at what you think is the right distance and then focusing, is rather hit-and-miss. More often than not you will be surprised to find that as the subject pops into focus, it is too large or too small in the frame. Remember that in close-up photography, changes of a few centimetres in working distance have a dramatic effect on image size. Moving the camera 5cm when shooting an insect portrait is like moving it several metres for a portrait of a person!

The best solution involves, once again, thinking in terms of image magnification rather than the distance between lens and subject. Pre-focus the lens to whatever magnification is appropriate to the subject. You can pre-focus on an inanimate object of similar size to the subject, but with experience you should find it possible to make an accurate enough guess as to the right magnification. With a macro lens, this can be set by making use of the scale of reproduction ratios marked on the lens barrel. With the focus correctly preset, you then move in on the subject with your eye to the viewfinder, and when it pops into focus it should be just the right size in the frame, so you can grab the shot immediately.

The TTL flash bracket approach is as near as you can get to point-and-shoot insect photography. My advice would be to use it when you need to, but don't seize upon it as a convenient way of avoiding having to carry a tripod!

Shield bug on bramble leaf. Because the shield bug and its surroundings are middle-toned, the TTL flash system has automatically produced a correct exposure.
105mm macro lens with 52.5mm extension tube, 1/250sec. at f/16 with flash.

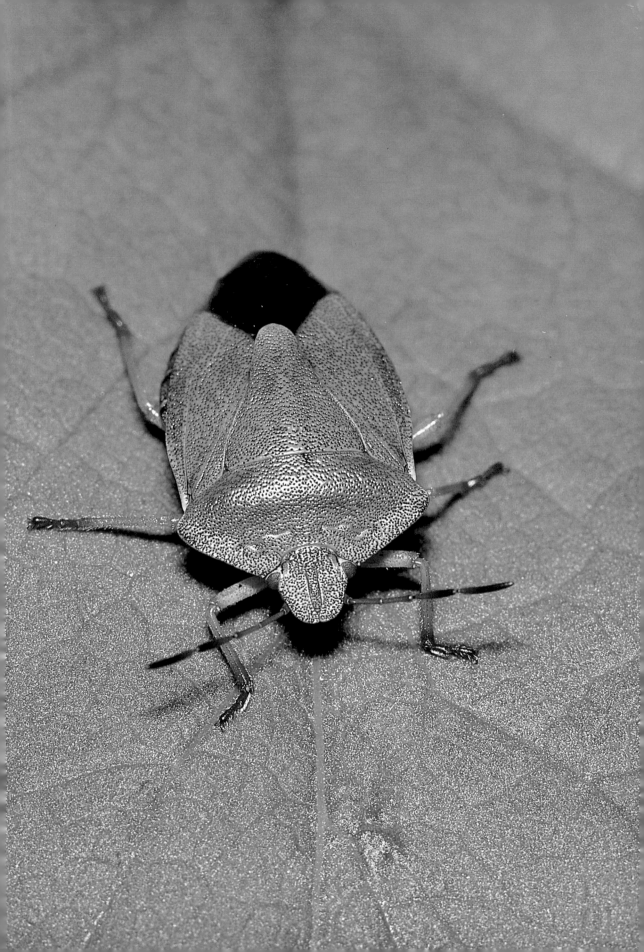

NATURAL LIGHT

MAKING THE MOST OF NATURAL LIGHT

If at all possible, I prefer to photograph insects using natural light, even though this can be quite a painstaking technique. Slow shutter speeds are the norm, so you need co-operative subjects, calm conditions, and a good tripod.

There is no point in trying this approach during the heat of a summer's day, because most insects will be too active and alert to remain still while a photographer sneaks up and positions a tripod. The last hour of light in the evening can provide better opportunities as insects settle to roost, but the best time to be out is at first light, when insects are still clinging to vegetation, and have been so chilled by the night air that they are unwilling or unable to move. Usually, this is also the calmest part of the day, and the time when the light is at its best.

Before the sun rises, there is a soft bluish light. Too diffuse to cast shadows, it is particularly flattering to pastel colours and fine detail. Later, with the first rays of the sun flooding the land, the light becomes very warm and directional, so it can highlight texture or produce some beautiful backlighting effects. It makes bright colours glow, and turns dewdrops into glistening jewels. Natural light has the potential to enhance your pictures enormously. The right kind of lighting can be the magic ingredient that will transform a respectable shot into something really outstanding.

Calm conditions are a prerequisite for natural-light work, because the slow shutter speeds which you must inevitably use don't offer any scope for freezing rapid movement. Anything stronger than an intermittent breeze is likely to set everything swaying to and fro, and thwart any attempt to shoot two-second exposures of roosting butterflies! If you do find yourself battling with the breeze, a third arm (see section on accessories), and/or a windbreak can sometimes save the day.

There is one other point to appreciate regarding the weather. This is that conditions in the evening and during the night are likely to determine how easy it is to find good subjects the following morning. If the evening is calm and

Damselfly on seedhead. This is an example of backlighting; the sun is behind the damselfly, and a lens hood was fitted in order to prevent it from shining directly into the lens and causing flare. The dark background, obtained by shooting towards the shadow of a nearby tree line, enhances the effect of the sunlight playing on the damselfly's wings. It also emphasises the outline of the seedhead.
180mm macro lens, 52.5mm extension tube, 1/30sec. at f/8.

dry, many insects will roost on exposed perches where they are easy to find and photograph. On the other hand, windy or wet weather will send them crawling for cover, and even though an overnight improvement may give you the impression that you are out on an ideal morning, worthwhile subjects will be impossible to find: they'll all be tucked away out of sight amongst dense vegetation. An awareness of this will save you a lot of fruitless early starts.

Assuming that you can find a subject, you must assess whether or not it will make a good picture. For a start it should ideally be sitting on something reasonably photogenic; a pristine scabious flower would certainly make a more pleasing addition to a shot than a mouldering nettle leaf.

Rather than see a good subject go to waste, I will sometimes move an insect from an unsightly perch on to something more aesthetically satisfying, but manipulating shots in this way is fraught with potential pitfalls. In particular, you must be careful not to set up a situation that would not occur naturally. Insects follow certain patterns of behaviour, and in most cases their choice of overnight resting place is not made at random. To a good naturalist, a badly set-up shot will look like a fake at once. I therefore restrict myself to setting up shots which I know occur naturally. For instance, having often seen marbled white butterflies resting on scabious flowers, I've set up similar shots of my own, but I've never found one resting on an orchid, so, tempting as it may be, I've never faked that one.

The other golden rule concerning the manipulation of subjects is that once you have your shots, you should return the insect to its original perch. This will ensure that you will not have interfered with its feeding or reproductive behaviour, and you won't have left it unduly exposed to predators.

Other factors to consider when assessing a possible shot are the lighting and the background. Unless there is some immediately obvious problem with either (perhaps you have a shaded subject against a sunlit background) it may be best to set up the shot first and then check the viewfinder. In order to find the best camera position I begin by moving around the subject, viewing it from different angles and paying particular attention to the way it is lit. Don't just look for the obvious frontlit shot, but consider whether the picture will be enhanced by sidelighting or backlighting.

Burnet Moths mating on scabious flower.
When subjects are abundant, don't rush from one to another trying to photograph them all. Be more selective. Eventually I found a perfectly situated pair. *105mm macro lens, 1/30sec. at f/8.*

Ermel moths mating on salad burnet. Finding small subjects tucked down in the grass is a knack which may take a little while to acquire. It's better to scan a small area slowly and thoroughly than to stride along trying to cover a whole meadow. 105mm macro lens with 52.5mm extension tube, 1sec. at f/11.

Mayflies are abundant subjects in waterside meadows. Like damselflies, they are long, slender subjects which don't fill much of the frame, so try to find one on a good perch. 180mm macro lens with 27.5mm extension tube, 1/15sec. at f/11.

Burnet Caterpillar and dew. The right kind of lighting can make a very average subject much more worthwhile. A heavy dew and some early morning sidelighting worked wonders for this burnet caterpillar. 105mm macro lens with 27.5mm extension tube, 1/4sec. at f/11.

Frequently, the angle at which you shoot is partly dictated by the need to make best use of a limited depth of field. In practical terms, this means ensuring that the plane of focus is aligned in such a way that the subject (or as much of it as possible) falls within the zone of acceptable sharpness.

The next step is to set up the tripod some distance away, in order to avoid disturbing the subject. With the camera set at about the right height, you can then move the whole lot carefully into position, and only a minimum of adjustment will be needed to arrive at the camera's final placement. Much as I like my trusty Benbo tripod, I wouldn't recommend setting one up from scratch in the midst of a thicket, and within inches of a precariously placed insect. In these circumstances, a Benbo will immediately acquire a will of its own and start flailing about like a set of animated bagpipes!

Once the shot is framed up, double-check the viewfinder for background hotspots and other unsightly elements which might spoil the picture. Also consider whether the lighting can be improved with a reflector or a diffuser; if so, a 'third arm' can be used to hold it in position.

Having set the exposure, the final consideration before shooting is wind movement. Even in quite still air, a frail plant stem will tremble occasionally from time to time. It's therefore essential to time each exposure to coincide with a moment when the subject is completely still. Take whatever steps you can to shield or steady the subject, keep your eye to the viewfinder, and if necessary be prepared to wait for several minutes between frames.

Because shooting with natural light can be a time-consuming process, you should not expect to return from an early morning session with dozens of first-rate pictures. Remember that it's unusual to have any more than two hours of good shooting before the light becomes too harsh and the insects become too active. If there is an abundance of potential subjects, don't rush from one to another trying to photograph them all. Be selective. Choose the best ones, and make a good job of photographing them.

One tip that will help you to make the most of what are usually short sessions: if possible, visit your chosen venue at dusk on the evening before your morning shoot and note the position of any well placed insects you can find. Usually they will still be there when you return in the morning, and you will not have to waste any time hunting for subjects; you can use all of it for actually photographing them!

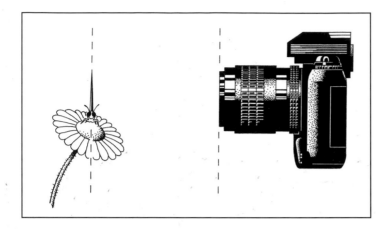

In order to make the most of a limited depth of field, you should align the camera so that the film plane and the main plane of the subject are parallel. The best way to check this before shooting is by viewing the subject and camera from the side, and then from above.

IN CONCLUSION

This book is as comprehensive as I could reasonably make it. I haven't omitted any 'secrets' or tricks of the trade, because I think making outstanding pictures is more a matter of adopting a sound technical approach and giving full rein to your own creativity. It is your creative input that is most likely to distinguish your pictures from the run of the mill, but don't forget that you won't be free to concentrate fully on this area until you have mastered the technical side of things, particularly the basics of exposure.

If you're striving for top-quality results, be honest in assessing your own work. Don't kid yourself that some basic defect in a picture doesn't really matter. If a picture is badly exposed, unsharp or poorly composed ask yourself where you went wrong and try to rectify the problem next time. Acknowledge your mistakes and learn from them. You shouldn't expect every shot to be perfect: it's normal to end up with a high percentage of rejects when shooting any form of wildlife in field conditions. I'd guess that about 80% of the frames I shoot end up in the bin for one reason or another.

One area which I couldn't cover in the space of these pages was the natural history of insects, quite an omission considering that, as a nature photographer, an intimate knowledge of your subject is one of the biggest advantages you can have. I suggest that you contact local naturalists' groups; membership of such a group will give you a head start in pinpointing good venues for photography, and may give you access to reserves which are out of bounds to the general public. You'll also meet people who will be willing to pass on some of their specialised knowledge.

In order to photograph this bumblebee, I set up the camera on the tripod, framed up a section of the foxglove and simply waited for a bee to fly into the shot. A 300mm lens enabled me to keep well back so that the bee wouldn't be deterred by my presence. It was about 7.30am on a bright June morning, and the light was strong enough to allow a shutter speed of 1/60s. This was just fast enough to freeze the movement of the bee. 300mm IF-ED lens with 52.5mm extension tube, 1/60sec. at f/8.

INDEX